TWIN SOUL ETERNAL LOVE

Anchoring the template for sacred relationships

Geraldina Lumezi

COPYRIGHT © 2017 by GERALDINA LUMEZI

The moral rights of the author have been asserted.

All rights reserved. No part of this book may be reproduced by any mechanical, photographic, or electronic process, or in the form of phonographic recording. Nor may it be stored in a retrieval system, transmitted or otherwise be copied for public or private use, other than for "fair use" as brief quotations embodied in articles and reviews, without prior written permission of the writer and publisher, in accordance with the provisions of the Copyright Act. Any person or persons who do any unauthorized act in relation to this publication may be liable to persecution and civil claims for damages.

Edited by: Elizabeth Stenson
www.thewriteway.ie

I will not bend or be put into a cage by those who think that the cage is the only place to be.

Geraldina Lumezi

I will find you

I will never forget, I promise that you will remain in me forever.
Until the last breath of the sun, the last play of the oceans,
 while there is life and laughter in me,
I will remember you.
As long as I have my dreams in the fields of eternity,
I will remember you always.
You are embedded in my veins,
every cell of mine breathes you.
Do you think love dies while we dream this life?
I will find you even when I am gone far,
far away behind the sun, under the sea,
 on top of the mountains.
Even when I am gone, my wandering soul will find you.
We will meet and you will know that it's me.
I will find you. I know.

I wrote this poem in 1993 when I was seventeen, prior to meeting my twin soul in the physical form.

This book is dedicated to my beautiful twin soul and to all beautiful souls who are in search of unconditional love.

Table of Contents

List of meditations..xi
List of invocation prayers (poems)..................................xxi

INTRODUCTION..1
FOREWORD..5

CHAPTER ONE

WHAT IS A TWIN SOUL CONNECTION?
Twin soul connection..11
Over-Soul..18
Soul Family..23
Soul Mates...26
Meditation: I am the creator of my own experience..................30
Invocation : My eternal Beloved...32

CHAPTER TWO

THE MEETING
-Temporary spiritual awakening-

The first initiation...35
The opening of the heart chakra...41
Feeling the 'lost' love..43
A glimpse of who you are..44
Meditation: Meet your Twin Soul...46
Invocation: I found you..48

CHAPTER THREE

THE PINK BALLOON PHASE

Tasting the divine love..51
Shaking of belief systems...54
Putting the love into a box and
healing your inner child...62
A glimpse of heaven..71
Meditation: Knowing and loving your inner child...............73
Invocation: Sacred love...74

CHAPTER FOUR

THE SEPARATION
-The runner chaser dynamic-

Missing the love...77
The soul pain..78
Don't explain yourself...83
Dissection of the ego...85
Meditation: Cutting cords for clearing the way to union.............87
Invocation: In each other all along...90

CHAPTER FIVE

THE EGO DROPS TO THE GROUND

Ego story...93
Suffering..95
Temporary awakenings...98
It is a journey..102
Meditation: Changing your beliefs...106
Invocation: Return to innocence...108

CHAPTER SIX

CRISIS AND THE TESTS OF ENDURANCE

Pushing and pulling energy..111
Synchronicities...116
Dark night of the soul and the awakening process....................119
The feeling of going crazy while awakening............................124
Meditation: Healing and balancing the chakras for divine union..127
Invocation: Feeling you...130

CHAPTER SEVEN

THE DANCE BETWEEN TWINS

Telepathic communication...133
Dream world and 'past lives'..137
Occasional meetings in the 3D...142
Rising of kundalini..143
Meditation: Feeling the connection and the unconditional love..146
Invocation: Love is all...148

CHAPTER EIGHT

COMPLETE SURRENDER OF EGO
-Surrender stage-
Seeing through the ego game...151
Sweet surrender and shadow side..154
Believing yourself..157
The heart way...158
Meditation - Exercise: Writing a letter to your ego..................160
Invocation: The unforgotten..162

CHAPTER NINE

RADIANCE OR COMING TO THE TRUTH

Claiming your truth..165
The charisma of radiance..168
Singing your song..171
The joy of living...172
Meditation: Radiating love from your sacred heart..................173
Invocation: Free to shine...174

CHAPTER TEN

HARMONIZING OR COMING TO THE SELF

Balancing the polarities..177
Feminine and masculine charge...179
Holding in the middle of the infinity sign (enlightenment)......183
Loving yourself completely...187
Meditation: Healing the body with your twin..........................189
Invocation: I see clearly..191

CHAPTER ELEVEN

THE LESSONS OF THIS CONNECTION

Your core experience..195
The interdependence of all life..197
Integrating all of your experiences...198
One love..200
Meditation: Meet your higher self...202
Invocation: The gift of love...204

CHAPTER TWELVE

THE MISSION

Giving this love to the world..207
It is not about you..209
Love wave...210
Higher frequency on earth...211
Meditation: Guardian angels of guidance and healing..............216
Invocation: My angel on earth..218

CHAPTER THIRTEEN

EMANATION AND FORCE OF UNCONDITIONAL LOVE

Changing the blood family template.................................221
Preparing the way for your children..................................223
Clearing the karma..226
Lapse of duality..227
Meditation: Forgiving your ancestors through unconditional love..228
Invocation: Coming home...231

CHAPTER FOURTEEN

SIGNING UP FOR THE ASCENSION OF PLANET EARTH

Awakening into the body..235
Knowing who we are..238
Living and breathing love...239
The God/Goddess truth...240
Meditation: Blessing the earth with happy healed humans.......241

Invocation: Fountain of love..244

CHAPTER FIFTEEN

HEALING THE EARTH

Giving the love vibrations to Earth..247
Closing the karmic soul contracts...249
The fragrance of new Earth..252
Living truly for each other...253
Meditation: Healing planet Earth..255
Invocation: One love...257

QUESTIONS AND ANSWERS..259
AFFIRMATIONS..271
ENDING NOTE..275
GLOSSARY..277
ABOUT THE AUTHOR...285

List of meditations

1. I am the creator of my experience..................30

2. Meet your twin soul........................46

3. Knowing and loving your inner child............73

4. Cutting cords for clearing the way to union...................87

5. Changing your beliefs.....................106

6. Healing and balancing chakras for divine union..........127

7. Feeling the connection and the unconditional love......146

8. Writing a letter to your ego...........................160

9. Radiating love from your sacred heart.........................173

10. Healing the body with your twin...............................189

11. Meeting your higher self 202

12. Guardian angels of guidance and healing...................216

13. Forgiving your ancestors through unconditional love...228

14. Blessing the earth with happy healed humans...........241

15. Healing planet Earth...255

List of invocation prayers (poems)

1. My eternal beloved 32

2. We found each other 48

3. Sacred love 74

4. In each other all along 90

5. Return to innocence 108

6. Feeling you 130

7. Love is all 148

8. The unforgotten 162

9. Free to shine 174

10. I see clearly 191

11. The gift of love 204

12. My angel on earth 218

13. Coming home 231

14. Fountain of love 244

15. One love 257

INTRODUCTION

Dear Reader and Beautiful Soul, I wrote this book firstly for the purpose of understanding myself and putting my own twin flame/soul experience into perspective, and secondly I wrote it for all of you who are struggling with this same experience of *Twin Soul* connection.

I wrote this book also for all of you who are searching for meaning in relationships with *Soul Mates* and want to experience sacred and beautiful relationships in life. This book is for all of you who are in search of unconditional love. As I wrote, I understood more of this journey and I began to put the pieces together like a magnificent puzzle of love. I have been on this journey for twenty-three years now at the time of writing this book, and I have poured all of my understanding, my learning, my wisdom and love into this creation.

If only one of you beautiful souls finds more understanding, or a little bit of comfort for your own twin soul journey, through this sharing of my experience, then I have fulfilled my mission. Also,

I wish for you to know that you are not alone in this experience because many of us have yearned for it too. This twin soul journey is not an easy one and this is why I decided to share it with you, because as we share our own experience, we may therefore benefit the many in their understanding of this deep soul love.

As we dare to share, we create a new reality together, because as much as this is an individual journey, it is at the same time a collective one. It is a shared wish of all of us to love and be loved for who we are; to learn how to love unconditionally. It is our collective wish to live a life with less pain and more compassion, less hate and more forgiveness, less aggression and more peace.

Twin souls are here to bring this love, by leading with example through living it first. Many twin souls are meeting now at this particular time in history to show the new way for all. They will set the *template* for all future relationships and show precisely what unconditional love is. For me personally, I met my twin twenty three years ago and this has been a long journey. I believe that in every true twin soul journey the experience may span decades, meaning that for this journey to unfold and union to take place, you need time. I am now in my *Illumination Phase* and carrying out my heart's mission.

I am teaching other twin souls how to align themselves with unconditional love so that they can step into their own mission and come into union. Dear Reader, I imagined this book to be alive and full of energy and I hope every word will speak to you personally. I tried with all my heart to make this complex journey as understandable as I could, as we all know how hard it is sometimes to find the right words to express what is of divine origin.

Each chapter contains a beautiful meditation to help you experience self-love firstly and then to experience the joy of union. At the end of each chapter I have created invocation prayers which are in the form of poetry and these will have a profound healing effect for your soul journey. You can say the invocations out loud, you can sing them or enjoy them in silence, but always let playfulness and joy be the key. Practice the meditations and say the prayers daily so that you can benefit and clear your energy for the time you will come into union.

At the end of the book is included one hundred beautiful affirmations which I have created to help to raise you into unconditional love as you practice them. I have also included a glossary explaining the meaning of the most frequently used terms, which initially appear in italic in the book, some of which may be unfamiliar to you.

At the back of the book are some questions and answers, which I chose from the most frequent questions I was asked about this soul journey. I hope that they clarify your questions and give you more illumination about this soul connection and your own personal journey.

Approach this twin soul journey as the route to coming back to your beautiful divine self, and ultimately to your twin. I hope this book will speak to you in the language of love and peace. With this said I wish you a beautiful journey through this book and I hope that you realize how beautiful you are. My wish is that all of us become one in this unconditional love and live it together.

From my heart to yours because we are one.

Love & Light
Geraldina Lumezi

FOREWORD

*"The desire and pursuit
of the whole is called love"*
Plato

Dear Reader and Beautiful Soul

Never before in the history of humankind have we as a collective consciousness or as one human soul been searching more to 'go home' or 'be home' with that special someone. We as the collective have signalled our desire for the Divine to read our hearts and to enable us to fulfil our missions, both individually and at the same time collectively, because what we do individually reflects onto all.

The twin soul concept is not new, just as there is nothing new on this Earth; we are rather remembering the forgotten and discovering the old knowledge in a new light. Throughout history people yearned for this *Unification of Soul*, for this 'other half'.

These unions were not possible before this era because the collective consciousness of humanity was not ready and awake to unconditional love. There was such deep conditioning and so many strong beliefs we needed to overcome that this soul love could not manifest fully under those circumstances. Although even in the most difficult of conditions people loved each other, twin soul connections usually ended tragically because society condemned them.

Twin soul connections always shook the status quo of beliefs about relationships as they tried to make space for the new way of relating among people.

Some of the twin souls throughout history are believed to be Jesus and Mary Magdalene, Tristan and Isolde, Isis and Osiris, Lancelot and Guinevere, and many more.

Many philosophers, mystics, and poets throughout history have spoken about the soul love connection, for example, Plato, Aristotle, Edgar Cayce, Sri Aurobindo, Sufi mystics and poets, and so the list goes on.

Plato described the twin soul union 2,500 years ago in his famous work Symposium:

> *"...and when one of them meets the other half, the actual half of himself, the pair are lost in amazement of love and friendship and intimacy and one will not be out of the other's sight even for a moment."*

His idea was that we were once whole and then we got divided into two and we live our lives in yearning for this 'other half' of ours, and when we find them, we feel complete again.

Greek philosopher Aristotle said:

> *"Love is composed of a single soul inhabiting two bodies"*

According to Greek mythology humans were created with four arms, four legs, and a head with two faces. Fearing their power, Zeus split them into two separate parts, condemning them to spend their lives in search of their other halves.

Edgar Cayce, who was also known as 'the sleeping prophet', in his historical description of Atlantis says:

> *" In the beginning the male and the female were as one, there lived in this land of Atlantis one Amilius who had first noted the separations of the beings, as inhabited that portion of the earth's*

sphere or plane of these peoples, into male and female separate entities or individuals".

Sufi spiritual writings from 800 years ago state:

"Out of the original unity of being there is a fragmentation and dispersal of beings, the last stage being the splitting of one soul in two, and consequently love is the search, by each half for the other half on earth or in heaven. As twin souls are so alike to begin with, it seems necessary for them to go their separate ways before they can complete each other. Identity and complementarity are the two driving forces and axes of love, for the complete being there must be blending of the two".

Sri Aurobindo, an Indian philosopher and yogi stated:

"Supreme state of human love is the unity of one soul in two bodies".

We live in a world of rapid awakening and many twin souls have been *embodied* together in this lifetime to help the *Ascension Process* on the planet, because at this point in time we can no longer be complacent. We are now conscious that we create and choose all of our experiences and that those choices have consequences.

We are aware of our own power and there is no going back to sleep again once you awaken. Be proud and be still so that you can hear your heart speaking the truth to you, and be ready and willing to step into it. We can only bring change to ourselves, to our families, to our communities and to our beautiful planet if we bring change into our lives individually.

By the grace and mercy of the *Divine Love* that we all are, we can manifest this new way of living into the tangible.

I believe in my heart and in my vision that this manifestation of love on earth is becoming more visible every day and each of us has a role to play in this Divine scenario. Spread your wings and fly, and shine brightly for all to see that there is nothing you would rather be and do more than love. Express that into the physical world so that everyone who comes to you drinks from your well.

This is our truth, our legacy and our new way. To shine brightly wherever we go and embody this soul love into the physical. Express yourself, be the love, breathe the love, live the love. It is true, it is true, and we are free at last.

We are free.

CHAPTER ONE

WHAT IS A TWIN SOUL CONNECTION?

" He's more myself than I am. Whatever our souls are made of, his and mine are the same".

Emily Bronte , Wuthering heights

"All your dreams can come true if you have the courage to pursue them".

Walt Disney

Twin soul connection

A twin soul connection is the strongest connection we can experience here on Earth. This connection is a deep spiritual soul love between 'two souls' whether they are embodied together on earth or not.

A twin soul is one soul which is embodied into two bodies whilst here on Earth. Twin souls have the same soul signature, the same soul frequency.

The soul 'split' happened due to experiencing life through two perspectives; the masculine and the feminine. Until both the masculine and the feminine begin to awaken and see this connection clearly, this connection is very painful, but at the same time spiritually, it is a very beautiful experience.
This connection cannot be broken or denied and cannot disappear, it goes on no matter what. This connection is not a romance from

the movies, walking in the moonlight holding hands without a care in the world. This connection is so much more.

For so many years we have been conditioned to think about love in a certain way, and here is this connection that shakes all of this conditioning. This twin soul experience rips us apart until we fall back into wholeness again; this connection is not an ordinary relationship, it is a spiritual connection, a union between 'two' souls. The deepest one you can imagine.

I believe that everybody is a twin soul, but not everybody is going to remember or *awaken* to that experience at the same time, and this is perfectly fine. We do not all have to choose the same experiences in this life in order to be in tune with our hearts. Indeed, for the evolution of our species, it would not be very practical for all of us to awaken at the same time. We each have a particular role to play and we are each equally important no matter what experiences we choose along the way.

*There are many paths on which to
awaken and they are all Divine.*

At this particular point of our evolution whilst living on this planet, many of us may wish to have this twin soul experience, to make the twin soul connection. But be careful what you wish for because this is a difficult journey and for those thinking 'I need my twin soul to make me happy because I am not complete enough in myself to feel happy', let me assure you that there are other, easier paths to being fulfilled.

To have a twin soul connection is very difficult and it is not a game. It is a spiritual experience and we as souls can have many different types of these experiences. Not everybody chooses the twin soul experience in this lifetime for themselves. You can have a very beautiful and satisfying experience with a soul mate, for example and in my opinion, many soul mate relationships can be sacred, if both partners are awake and striving for harmony.

Still, soul mate relationships are different from twin soul union. Twin souls are usually not permanently together until the final union. They experience these 'mini unions' as I like to call them, coming back and forth to each other until the final union happens. What they have between them is not a classic relationship, what they have is union. Your twin soul is you, the other side of the coin, but still the same coin.

When the eternal knowing and bliss of love happened, or when the soul divided into two, there remained two opposite polarities which are magnetized strongly. Even if you erase all the concepts, all the names and labels we give to this connection, you can feel the magnetic pull towards your twin. When you awaken and get to know your twin, there will be no confusion, either the connection is there or it is not.

You cannot wish for this connection to be there from your head, it is there in your heart. One of the strong characteristics of twin souls is the magnetic pull between them and no matter what they do or whether they try to break this strong bond, the bond between them is unbreakable and it will remain.

So when people ask me how they will know if they have a twin soul, I tell them to throw all the labels out of the window and just feel if they have this strong pull towards another. You cannot miss that.

Twin souls are not two halves of one soul but two whole souls of the same soul, holding everything in that 'half' and nothing is missing.

I can compare this to the hologram. The hologram holds all the information of the whole, even the smallest part of the hologram has the same information as the whole. It is a contradiction and a paradox but such is the whole twin soul experience. Twin souls are one always through eternity, they only go their separate ways to come back together again, and an infinity sign in a heart shaped bond is always there until they choose a lifetime where they want to experience reunion again.

A soul is not tied to the earth and can do unimaginable things for the mind, and the twin soul connection is here to show us that nothing is impossible for the soul. There is no distance, no time passing; no limit or dimensions that love cannot endure, conquer, and get through.

We all remember in our soul the time of 'separation' from *Source*, thus from ourselves, and we carry that pain inside, that longing. Our soul is merely a spark of God's light that we received for this life experience. This cosmic love is here in the flesh and is a living proof that we are never separated, we are in each other all the time. Throughout the twin soul journey twins help each other to heal and lead each other to God/Goddess consciousness so they could see clearly their divinity. This is how powerful and beautiful this connection is.

This is a celestial love brought to earth to illustrate to us what love can do and create.

Love can only create miracles and beauty.

Through this twin soul journey we see the force of love, the unconditional endless endurance, patience, and the rain of mercy and understanding that love offers us. On this journey you will be shaped like a diamond in the rough into compassion, patience, unconditional love and the embrace of Divinity.

You will be reshaped out of all your old beliefs about life and yourself, into a complete new you.

This journey gives you the touch of magic in the everyday, the mystical experience of Divine Love, the unity of your own soul in beauty and heart space.

If you choose not to meet your twin in the physical body in this lifetime, know that your twin can also exist in other realms of reality and give you strength here on earth. They are always with you.

For you who did not meet your twin soul in the physical form or if you have a twin in other realms, you can always connect to them through meditation and prayer. When we live a life from the sacred space of the heart, we enter another kind of dimensional reality where the rules of physicality do not apply any more. In this reality you can touch, hear, speak, and feel your twin any time you wish.

Signs of meeting a twin soul:

1. SOUL RECOGNITION
When you meet your twin you will have a deep soul recognition. You know them even if you have just met them. You recognize their eyes, voice and their soul frequency. You have a feeling of complete safety and familiarity. Your presences will speak to each other. It's a feeling of returning 'home'. You know that the search is over.

2. LOVE AT FIRST SIGHT
You will feel a deep love and a strong bond instantly. Inexplicable intimacy even if you just met them. This deep love feels ancient.

3. UNUSUAL MEETING
The environment and the way you meet is unusual. You will be both doing something which you usually don't do. Synchronicities will play a big part in your meeting and the meeting will be synchronized by the Divine.

4. SEPARATED BUT CONNECTED
When separated both twins feel soul pain, emptiness and loneliness like nothing can fulfil them, all while being connected telepathically.

5. TELEPATHIC CONNECTION
Twin souls know each other's thoughts, your twin knows what you think even before you say it. You can finish each other's sentences and use the same expressions as each other in conversations. When separated you have full telepathic conversations with each other.

6. SYNCHRONICITIES TO KEEP YOU ON A PATH
When you meet your twin you will experience so many synchronicities that you will not be able to ignore them.
You will be 'bombarded' with them.

7. DREAM VISIONS
Twin souls communicate a lot through dreams and if you are a twin soul you are going to visit each other in dreams. You will share thoughts, heal, and be with each other. You will astral travel in dream states and acknowledge that separation is illusion.

8. SPIRITUAL AWAKENING
When you meet your twin soul for the first time you are going to become aware of yourself, you will feel like you are 'born' again. As the journey progresses they are going to 'push' you out of your ego conditioning into your soul awakening and healing.

9. AWAKENING SIXTH SENSES
As you progress on your twin soul journey your extrasensory perception heightens, and all of the sixth senses start to awaken.

10. 'PAST LIVES' TOGETHER

You will remember your 'past lives' together and they will be clues to your union. You will heal, learn and understand your union through them and they will help to integrate your experiences.

11. MISSION OR DIVINE PURPOSE

Both twins will have a spiritual desire to help people, to work for a cause. They will feel they have a purpose to fulfil together as a team. If they realize this desire their talents 'explode' in the best way for them to complete the mission.

12. NO TABOOS BETWEEN THEM

They can talk about anything for hours and there are no barriers between them. There is a feeling of intimacy, openness, and oneness.

13. SOUL ATTRACTION

They will be very attracted to each other, not only physically but on a soul level. With twins, souls do literally attract. It feels like making love with your twin is truly sacred, more like a religious spiritual act that expresses the love they feel for one another.

14. FEELING OF COMPLETION

When you are with them you feel like you are complete, like finally nothing is missing in life. You feel like you could 'conquer the world' when they are beside you. They give you strength and motivation.

Through our evolving as humans in relationships we experienced a bodily love, we loved from the body, we experienced a heart love, we loved from the heart, but now is the time to experience the higher love from the soul, soul love.

Over-Soul

In the beginning of creation, we were in the light and of the light, before we were made to go and experience physical form. The formless wished to see and feel what form is, and how it would be to experience this *duality*.
We were created in this perfection, in the perfect image of the Mother/Father. We have inside of us the divine Mother/Father essence in our consciousness for eternity. Their love is a play of light; the shades of light dancing and exploring, their playful love kissing us endlessly and creating us in beauty.

Love is a constant creation of the new and wonderful and we are created in this perfection, out of love and joy. This world is but a reverie of love from out of the heart of the God/Goddess.

You could say that it is we who wish for something, and in that wishing the Divine expands more and becomes more of itself through us. All of existence and creation is interconnected and we were never truly separate from our Divine essence. The divine Mother/Father went further into their love ecstasy, and created little particles of light and fire that we call souls.

Soul is the spiritual principle of human beings, and in many religions it is said to be the incorporeal and immortal essence of a living being.

All souls come from one bigger cluster of light; we will call it *Over - Soul*, that is, the spiritual unity of all beings. This energy is the one life force that unites us all, a spiritual essence and a vital force, which transcends individual consciousness.

Underneath all the layers of conditioning we know deep down that we are from one source of creation, and whatever names we give to that creation do not matter; the one thing that matters is that we are conscious of our origin. For example, we each have our individual consciousness but looking at life from the perspective of unity, a person, a dog, and a tree are all spiritually connected.

You can imagine the Over-Soul as an endless pool full of light and our souls as little sparks of the same light. Our Divine Mother/Father continued playing a bit further and liked the idea of one soul spark splitting in two in order to experience the *three dimensional reality (3D)*, from the perspective of two bodies.

When two twin souls decide to incarnate on earth they can have different experiences but their experiences are from the same template. A template is a pattern or an overlay of experiences, which will bring them closer to what they want to learn here on the earth plane. They have the same blueprint, same set of tasks to fulfil, it does not really matter which road they choose to take, their goal is to find home and each other. I saw this truth in my own inner vision, and cried the tears of joy and beauty of what we are; we are an indescribable beauty.

We are these co- creators of the Divine will, and if we align ourselves with this, our lives will be a living proof of heaven on earth.

There is a beautiful story, a legend that says ; "In the moment that spirit enters our human vehicle called body, our guardian angel kisses us on the forehead and puts his finger in the crease where our lip and nose touch, and sings us a song. Our soul song is like a signature song for us, and during a lifetime we are going to hear it at some point and 'wake up and remember'. When the angel's finger touches us, we forget this truth as we enter Earth". We came into this plane of existence with amnesia, which serves us well, and when we wish to wake up we start to remember again.

Waking up or enlightenment is nothing more than remembering the truth of who we are.

The twin soul experience is going to feel a lot of the time like you know something deep in your soul but cannot remember. As you evolve in your journey you are going to remember more and more. Everything is vibration in this Universe, vibrating at certain frequencies, and these frequencies manifest as sounds, words, and images. Sound is the creative vibration and has a tremendous amount of energy in it. When each soul wanted to experience other realities, a song (a specific sound) was created for that soul so that it can remember who it is and where it originated from. It can be said that twin souls have the same signature song of their souls and when they meet they hear that music in each other.

Twin souls have the same vibratory frequency and when they meet, they unconsciously pick up this frequency from each other.

Over-Soul is the stream of energy fuel for how you express yourself in any reality you choose. Over-Soul is the one-source stream from which soul families originate, and from where we draw our life force and energy. When twin souls wished to separate into this dimensional reality for the joy of experience, the eternal connection (the loop of infinity) always remained, to remind them of the connection.

Twin souls represent one soul spark, one energy stream of consciousness to experience that single point of consciousness from two bodies. They are the polar opposites of the same soul frequency; the yin and the yang.

They are the feminine and the masculine charge of one soul which chose to incarnate into two bodies. One of them represents the masculine charge and the other the feminine charge, in this beautiful dance of balancing. At the beginning of the split, on embarking on the experience, we remembered our former eternal bliss and it is due to the sadness of this split that we yearn so much for this unification throughout our life on earth. We could never forget even through centuries of experiencing that union with self. This is the core of what twin souls represent on earth. They represent the coming home to each other into union and serving the whole world with this energy, this potent third energy of unconditional love. They set the template for future relating on this planet. When they come back to each other in their physical form, they embody this Godlike quality in their love.

*Twin souls bring in Christ's consciousness
through their love.*

Underneath all of the layers of conditioning, we know who we truly are; it is just that we forgot for a while and we need to remember that we wished for this to be so. We are not victims in the scenario of life, we are the masters of our experience, and when we remember who we are, nothing just happens to us anymore, it rather happens as we ordain it.

*Self-mastery is the acknowledgment that we are the embodied
Divine in the eternal play of consciousness.*

Why would we think we are anything less? In the space and time of our current reality it is important that we remember our origins. Remember who we are, and where that heart space is (the kingdom of God) that we are looking for. Jesus said this clearly: 'The kingdom of God is in you' and he meant it is literally in your heart and soul, and not somewhere external.

I have to admit that sometimes language cannot do justice to spirituality and to our mystical feelings and experiences. I love words and playing with them, I love writing, but sometimes I feel that language is a poor interpretation of what is truly wordless. Nonetheless, I will try to bring this light and beauty to you with every word I use. We know that God/Goddess dwells in the silence and in the wordless space.

The field where all possibilities exist is a field of silence and instant realization.

You must understand that we are firstly created in our soul where all possibilities lie and then we chose to be manifested on the earth plane. The planet we live in is just one of many in our galaxy. Just because we cannot travel at the speed of light yet, it does not mean that other species and living planets do not exist. In our third dimensional perception of space and time, it is very hard to grasp the intelligent forces of such magnitude. Time and space in other realities don't exist the way we perceive them. Everything is contained in the now flow, with no linear time line of past, present, or future. I have worked with many people as a past life regression therapist and through my own experience and my clients' experience I have learned that past lives are not past as we perceive them, but rather live in us the same as our future lives do.

All the possibilities live in us and for us in the eternal NOW.

The present moment is the only moment where time does not exist. It is true that when we enter this three dimensional reality we experience a sort of amnesia of the totality of who we are, for our own benefit while we are here on earth. We have our limited five senses for a good reason but we have our sixth sense and other senses so we can use them for better navigation.

When you awaken from the illusion of a dream, you start to experience everything in your own unique way. You start to be your own authority, your own guru, your own director of reality.

It is the purpose of twin soul experience to awaken you to your soul and beauty and to awaken all of your dormant senses, beyond the five you use here in this reality.

Soul Family

A *Soul Family* is a heavenly version of the family of souls; group of souls who wish to share experiences by interacting with each other and who can choose to incarnate together here on earth.

We do not merely live here on earth but we complete our duties and tasks simultaneously on higher dimensions.

Soul mates can come from our soul family or other different soul families, depending on what contract you have made regarding what you wished to experience for yourself. A soul family, as you can imagine, is like the family you have on this earth, whose experiences in other dimensional realities are similar with complementary tasks and goals to achieve. We interact here on the earth plane in a similar way as we do in higher dimensions. We exist in the realms of other realities simultaneously. Your soul family members can be embodied together with you or exist only in other dimensions to help and guide you through the earth journey.

Consciousness is not restricted and bound by time, and we can experience parallel lives and can be at many places at the same time.

When you start to awaken from this three dimensional plane of consciousness you start to receive all the help you need to see into who you are, in a deeper sense. You clearly see that this reality is not the only one.

Your soul family members start to communicate with you and guide you and help you in your life. When you start to awaken to your higher self-awareness, you receive guidance for your highest manifestation on earth. In other words your soul family and your spiritual guides, your guardian angels, love you so much that they help you and guide you to fulfil your highest potential. At this point in time, we are meeting more and more people from our close soul family to precipitate our missions. In this new reality, you may feel that you need to move away from certain people, even close friends whom you have known all your life, because they don't vibrate the same as you anymore.

At the same time you might meet new people and do wonders with them as a team because you are on the same vibration frequency. You will feel that you have known these people forever, even if you know little or nothing about their current lives and you have met them only a short time ago. This will happen more and more because we need these soul tribes to come together, helping each other and raising the collective consciousness so that we can change the present condition of life on this planet.

Keep in mind that people who vibrate at very different vibration frequencies cannot stay together. You and your soul mates support, challenge, and push each other for mutual growth. When you compare soul mate relationships with twin soul experiences you will usually feel like something is missing, even if you have a less challenging relationship and perceive it as harmonious according to three dimensional relating. We are experiencing the twin soul journey in the first place to find that 'missing part of the puzzle', which is firstly our self-love, then our union with divinity and finally with our twin.

We are not aware of this truth while we are playing this out. It is a game of hide and seek going on for ages and it is perfect in its imperfection, but I think in this time of awakening we know better.

In a soul mate relationship the other person is reflecting only a part of you, and you need to bring your attention to that to resolve and embrace it. In a twin soul connection your twin reflects the whole of you so you can deal with it all and there cannot remain any part that is hidden.

That is why this union is so overwhelming and challenging, because no matter how you try to push it away or escape it, the reflection remains, for the final revelation. It is not easy when you see all of the sides of your character reflected through your twin, it is very intense. This union feels like God/Goddess is pushing you into your soul essence so that you can shine bright like the diamond that you are. As I often say you can 'escape' from any soul mate relationship but from your twin there is no way out, the only way 'out' is inwards.

The way out of pain is in your deepest soul search.

Soul family is very real and exists even if you do not believe it, and when you meet somebody from your soul family, you instinctively just know each other.
You don't need any earthly details from them such as where they went to school, or what they like or dislike. When you meet somebody from your soul family you know them and recognize them on a deeper level. At the same time you know that you are creating something with them from a higher dimensional awareness.
I believe that we as humans are not fully incarnated here on earth and that our soul exists in other dimensional realities simultaneously and is en route to integration. Your soul family can

also help you from a higher dimensional reality and talk to you through your intuition, meditation, and dreams. They love you very much and support you all the way. You are never alone on this earthly journey.

You are always loved even when you experience the hardest times and do not believe in life any more.

When you awaken, you start to meet more and more people from your soul family, or from your planets of origin. Many twin souls were incarnated on highly evolved planets such as the Pleiades and Sirius star systems, and hence, they experienced the bliss of living in harmony. When they were assigned to earth, they never forgot that bliss and they always try to recreate it here on earth. That is why they are the earth angels bringing forth this love for everybody to see.

Soul Mates

A soul mate is a soul who will help you complete a certain task you set for yourself and play that role perfectly for you, as you would for them. They may come from the same soul family or a different soul family, it all depends on what you initially agreed upon. As we journey through our life, we connect with quite a few people, whom I call soul mates (mates of the soul, aka travelling mates).
We all have approximately 12-15 soul mates throughout our lives and they can be our friends, family members, work colleagues, children, partners, acquaintances, and these relationships can be very loving.
A few decades ago we believed that we have only one soul mate but since then that understanding evolved as we did.

Now the term 'soul mate' has evolved into the concept of twin flame or twin soul, meaning that your ultimate soul mate is your twin soul.

Even if you are not on the twin soul journey, we are evolving from head based relationships to soul based relationships in general.

All of us we want to be truly seen. This is the primordial feeling of ecstasy, of intimacy, passion and love. When you are dealing with a soul mate karmic relationship there is almost always an invisible border present limiting you to where you can go with exploring yourself. That border manifests as a certain set of lessons you have to master. When you are with a karmic soul mate that emptiness is inevitable because your soul knows and wants to dive more deeply into itself but at the same time it can't because there are limitations in the form of karmic issues.

With soul mates and karmic partners even sexuality is limited because it comes from the assumption that the body can give pleasure. Yes, the body can give us pleasure, but with twin souls this physical pleasure will never be 'enough', because they make love with their energy bodies where they always dive deeper with their souls into the act of making love. Only then is there the potential for the eternal ecstasy of self-knowing to happen. When you wake up to your divine self you see clearly, you can even instinctively feel and know how long the soul contracts between you and your soul mates are going to last.

As you observe yourself more consciously, you see that the disharmony you experience in the outer circumstances is actually the disharmony in your belief system and your views on life in general.

You see clearly what lessons you needed to learn to integrate into each particular relationship. No relationship is a mystery anymore; your soul knows all the writings of all of your lives and your heart. If you are awake and in the moment, they are like the writings on the wall, which you can actually see and feel if you are conscious enough to read for yourself and your soul mates. We really do have soul contracts and we need to proceed to the completion of the same.

In order to complete a contract, you need to be very conscious of yourself and integrate your learning's, because otherwise other soul mates will present themselves to you to repeat the task again. That is why people end up in the same kinds of relationships with the same difficulties, in unsatisfying jobs or situations. It feels like you hit the repeat button over, and over again.

This happens because as humans we try to avoid the lesson, or escape the mirror, and we cannot escape the mirror. You'll end up finding another one again and again, until you give up and face yourself. Such is the playfulness and the creativity of our souls.

We are not in the world, the world is in us and it reflects everything we need to see in order to accept and become the love that we are.

We came here on earth to experience life through duality and contrast and through experiencing duality we expand and evolve. Through darkness, we know our light; through anger we come to peace; through oppression we are liberated, and can experience freedom. When you are done with your task of learning a certain lesson, you will know in your heart that you have finished. It will feel like a weight has been lifted from your heart and mind and you will feel freer. So in order to summarize and without getting confused with the terminology, let us just reiterate:

We have God/Goddess-(Mother/Father Divine parents the feminine and the masculine creation energy) the Over-Soul from where all souls emanated, soul families which are a group of kindred spirits, individual souls, and then 'split' souls or twin souls. I must emphasise that this is put in this hierarchical order merely to enable our conceptualized understanding of the subject, but in spiritual and celestial truth, there are no hierarchies and no individual souls exist, because everything is divine consciousness playing a beautiful game of love and creativity. Now you are probably trying to grasp this with your conscious mind, but do not try to understand the depth of the ocean with a teaspoon. The ocean of life is too big and too mysterious. Instead try to release the grip of the mind to want to know everything and just feel in your heart's consciousness the truth of your existence.

The mystery of life is inexplicable and if you are conscious of this mystery it will reveal the beauty it holds in unison with your surrendering to the wisdom of your heart. Life is not lived in order to understand it but to accept and appreciate its mystery.

We only perceive our individuality when we become embodied here, and we think that we are separate for that part of our earth experience, when in reality, we are just a wave in the ocean. We fool ourselves by acting separately for a while and then we awaken to the truth that we are the ocean and have never been separate in the first place.

My question is that when we decide to leave this reality (when we die) do we not melt into united consciousness again? Our 'individual' existence is a very intelligent game and that is why we have created our beautiful egos as a tool to play it all out. How would we play our roles if we did not set our egocentric selves to act accordingly? The only thing is that we forgot what we have created and got caught up in this game, and the stories that we tell ourselves along the way. It is very funny and childlike when we come to understand it from this point of view.

I think that we are all collectively coming out of our human childhood into a more mature state of being and understanding that we have had our freedom all along but for us to conserve this freedom we must be willing to let go of our conditioning and programming.

We must be willing to grow up spiritually and become responsible human beings. It appears that we have collectively been under mass hypnosis and we are now waking up to create something new for ourselves. We are waking up out of our illusions. The final rise up is here for all of us.

Meditation
I am the creator of my own experience

The purpose of this meditation is to bring you into the awareness of what you are creating in this existence. It gives you the possibility to observe yourself from a higher perspective of creation. It gives you the peace to relax into your potential, a sense of diving into your divine right of creating abundance in every field of your life.

Find a calm and peaceful space where you can relax for a while without being disturbed. Relax your body by sitting or lying down, whichever feels more comfortable. Close your eyes and begin by breathing and consciously observing your breath as it comes in and out of your nose.
With every deep breath, you will relax more and more, until all of the outer sensation becomes quiet and you dive into your inner being. You are calm and peaceful. You feel like the calm glassy surface of a lake.
In your inner eye, see yourself standing in front of a screen. Imagine this screen like a large television, look at the screen, and notice that as images start to appear, you see your life as it is at this moment. Now stop for a while and observe these images. As the images start to circle, you see your relationships, your job, your body, your health.

Maybe you won't like what you see but just be the observer of this, do not attach any emotion to these images, just observe as if this is somebody's else life and accept whatever comes. Everything is clear to you, as you observe. See yourself truly, where you are at this point in your life. You are watching your own life on a screen as if it is a movie. Accept what you see and embrace what it is with love. As you observe and see your creation, see and feel what you would like to change, make mental notes of what you want to do differently. Feel which scene you would like to change.

Now go to the screen and switch the screen off. When you do this you give your subconscious mind the message that you are unplugging and disconnecting from these images. Now, go and plug the screen on again and as you do this, see the new life of yours. The images start to appear but this time you see what you want to create next. You are completely aware of your role in consciously creating your life.

You are a screenwriter, a director and the main actor in your movie called 'life'. Now observe again and see new scenes, new relationships, maybe a new job you wish to do, your body full of health and glowing, material things you wish to attain. There is no limit to what you can create. See yourself smiling from your heart and being at peace with your renewed life. See your face glowing with what you have created. Lock these new images into your heart, because you manifested them just now, and they are true. So be it.

Say this aloud to your subconscious mind;

'I am a powerful creator of my own life and I can create with my heart and my soul intention, and so it is. Amen'.

Invocation
My eternal Beloved

Oh my Beloved of this eternal love
the time of recognition has come,
as we always intended in our beautiful souls.
The recognition of what we truly are,
you in me and me in you, two of the same.
Two expressions of divine but one eternal flow of love.
Eternal my Beloved you are to me,
like the scent of the sea is to the wave.
Like the beautiful shine of the moon to the night,
you light up my path, so I can walk safely.
There you are caressing me without effort, feeling me.
We meet in the fields of dreams and dance together.
Each night our fires ignite again in the subtle dance of our breath.
We wished for this life.
I know you I know myself, I know myself I know you.
I love you I love myself, I love myself I love you.

CHAPTER TWO

THE MEETING
-Temporary spiritual awakening-

' It's clear to me now that I have been moving toward you and you toward me for a long time. Though neither of us was aware of the other before we met , there was a kind of mindless certainty bumming blithely along beneath our ignorance that ensured we would come together. Like two solitary birds flying the great prairies by celestial reckoning, all of these years and lifetimes we have been moving toward one another.

Robert James Waller, Bridges of Madison County

*"Lovers don't finally meet somewhere.
they are in each other all along".*

Rumi

The first initiation

In twin soul connections there are various scenarios, in the same way that there are different people experiencing the connection. We are all individuals here on earth, therefore we do not all wish for the same things. There are no fixed rules in these connections but there are some similar reference points and stages for all experiencing this connection.

From my own experience, I can divide this journey into several stages or phases. Remember that the stages do not have to be fixed in a particular order for everybody, they are just reference points for you to map what is happening throughout your journey.

As I said before, each twin soul journey is unique, and as you go through it, you can come and go, in and out of different stages. When you think that, for example, you are in the *Surrender Phase* and have worked so hard on yourself, you may then experience another layer of surrender or come in and out of the *Radiance Phase*. You can go deeper into surrender and realise that every time you think you have arrived somewhere, this journey pushes you deeper.

My advice to you is to just relax and take this journey day by day and trust that your twin soul journey is unfolding as it is supposed to in perfect harmony and divine timing.

Stages of the Twin Soul Journey:

1) Meeting your twin soul
2) Pink balloon phase
3) Separation - Runner/chaser dynamic
4) Crisis and the tests of endurance
5) Surrender
6) Radiance
7) Harmonizing and coming into union

Each stage has a purpose. When it comes to meeting your twin soul, the environment and the way in which the meeting happens is always unusual. When we think about when it happens it is always certainly when we least expect it consciously.

This meeting is deliberately arranged by divine timing to awaken you at that particular moment and if you knew already that you would meet your twin it wouldn't have the same impact on your temporary awakening. There is always some leeway for interpretation in what I have just stated here, because in the end it all depends on what you wished for yourself in your soul contract. The most important thing throughout this journey is not to compare your journey with other twin soul experiences, because you may get discouraged if some experiences differ.

You have to trust yourself and compare others' twin soul experiences only as an additional help on your journey. Everything I speak about is from my own twin soul journey and how I perceive this in my own reality.

When we are living in spirit and truth there are no set rules unlike when we are bound by our egos. Spirit is ever flowing and revealing, thus in the twin soul journey you flow and learn constantly. The so-called stages can last longer or shorter as it all depends on how you awaken through them. And one thing that this journey teaches you is that there are no beliefs that you cannot question, and tomorrow you may change everything and start all over again. It teaches you not to cling to anything, it teaches you to flow with your spirit and your spirit is unpredictable.

The ego is predictable and takes us on the same road always, but when it comes to the spirit, we have to surrender to the flow.

The twin soul journey is so difficult due to its unpredictability and the way it asks for all of your trust; it asks you to jump into the unknown.

The meeting of your twin is an out of this world feeling; you stand there in soul recognition even though you may not be aware of it consciously at the time, but after some time passes you will become aware of what exactly happened at the time of the meeting. It is a feeling of returning home after a long journey, a feeling of familiarity and safety that you cannot explain to yourself, that warmth around the heart space. It is instant soul recognition of something lost a long time ago. As I said previously you will not be completely conscious of that at the time of meeting your twin until you look at it in retrospect much later. This is because this will be only a temporary awakening and not the complete remembering of your twin. You will sense this nagging feeling of restlessness as if all of a sudden you have lost your 'peace'. You have not lost your peace but you do not like the feeling of your soul being disturbed, and this meeting stirs your soul. It awakens you if only for a second. It touches you. This occurs because it is only a temporary touch of this love, it touches you like a beautiful breeze and you are left standing there in amazement, asking yourself what just happened.

In my experience of meeting my twin soul, the thing I knew very strongly at the time was that something was pulling me towards this person but I could not put it in to perspective then, although it was so strong that I could not ignore it. I call this the first *Initiation of Soul* and you are never the same after this experience. You can easily divide your life into before and after the encounter of meeting your twin soul.

What the first initiation means is that this is the first soul shock that almost feels like an electrical shock has passed through you. It is the beginning of a long journey into your own Self.

Both twins will start to experience an acceleration of spiritual understanding and growth after their initial meeting.

The place and circumstances of meeting are normally unusual. You may meet unexpectedly in the emergency room in a hospital, or you may accidently drop your books and have somebody pick them up for you, you could fall down in the street and that person may help you to get back up. When twin souls are destined to meet the Universe can get very creative, trust me. The synchronicities work here at full speed to assist the meeting to occur.

My personal experience of meeting my twin soul happened when my family and I were moving house and we needed somebody to help us move and load the furniture. My cousin who was in the army at that time asked this person to come with him to help, and that was the day when my life changed. I met my twin when I was a seventeen year old teenager living in my own world of music, high school, and family issues. At the time my father had left to work in another country and my mother was considering a divorce. It was a mess.

I was as angry as any teenager can be at seventeen, attending high school amid all the traumas of being a teen and questioning everything. Still I was happy in the way that every teen is in this period of growing and adolescence when you should be as free as possible. I was not expecting this meeting in a million years, but trust me the divine intelligence is very creative when it decides to put two people together who are destined to meet.

Sometimes it can be very funny, but meeting your twin soul can be never expected and planned consciously, so there's no point in deciding to go out and meet your twin or search for a boyfriend.

This meeting is pre-planned, but on a soul level, therefore it is an unconscious process until it wakes you up completely. I got up that day and started helping my family to pack and prepare for the arrival of the truck. When my cousin arrived with him, I shook hands with this person and I can remember as today, my whole body lit up like a Christmas tree. It was a rush of adrenalin and movement in the body, which I could not explain to myself at the time, but I know now that the *kundalini* life force was moving. It was some sort of deep recognition, a memory of something past. We met and were introduced to each other and from the first glance into his eyes I stood there and had a complete feeling of familiarity around this young man, we didn't even have to speak. I felt that our presences felt and spoke to each other. This feeling was completely new to me. It was the strangest feeling and the most beautiful at the same time, and I can only describe it like the safest feeling in the world. It felt like coming home after many years, from a long journey and now I was finally safe. Like I had been in some sort of pain and now I felt all this relief after the pain subsided.

As we carried these boxes, he sang to me under a window, he was not reserved at all; we behaved like we had known each other intimately for a long time and we were just continuing where we had left off. It all felt so natural. I remember my inner thinking back then, when I was wondering how I can feel this if we have only just met. On that day, my heart started a million step journey of remembering who I am.

It is so funny that we expect something so dramatic when it comes to meeting our destiny and usually it is something we do not even recognize in that moment, because our destiny unfolds from our spirit, not our mind.

Of course, I did not know that consciously, at that moment. Remember that when you are operating from the ego perspective you do not recognize something as amazing as this experience right away. The ego is not equipped for this knowing, our ego awareness does not know a thing about true love.

As the story unfolded, I began to feel things I never knew existed. Firstly, I felt that I loved this person, but it was not a feeling of only falling in love but a kind of a deeper love and this love felt ancient. The love I felt was old, meaning that it had been going on for a long time. Through our energies I sensed this strong bond, the magnetic pull toward this person. Your twin soul is going to enter your world like an angel feather lightly and then become the greatest storm that you have ever experienced. There is always an element of surprise in it.

You do not wake up one morning with the thought; 'I am going to meet my twin soul today', it does not function that way. For this experience to occur, the souls will have made an agreement a long time before.

For twin souls, when the time for meeting comes everything conspires to bring them together. Synchronistic events surround this union at all times, and are a big part of this journey. As you progress you will experience many amazing synchronicities to keep you on your path.

This path of twin soul journeys did not come out of nowhere; you ordained this path way a long time before, together with your twin. This mission starts way before you become conscious of it and it may even be 'recognized' in childhood.

In my own experience, I felt this path even when I was a child, I kept thinking that I was made for someone, and that someone was

out there waiting for me. A feeling that somebody the same as me was out there in the world, a boy who was identical to me, like a twin.
I always had a feeling that nothing could ever fulfil me until I found this love that was calling to me, this person. This was a burden to me because I was only a child, and did not understand this feeling. It was a lonesome feeling, I felt so alone. It was a yearning, a missing, sometimes a torture, and sometimes a bliss, each time I felt this love overwhelming me. I was very sensitive as a child and could feel and perceive myself and other people very deeply. I knew there was something special about this feeling, but of course, I did not know at the time what it was.

The opening of the heart chakra

When you experience that heart warmth, the fluttering, the skipping of a beat, this is actually the *heart chakra* expanding and taking more light in. In that first initiation phase, you will feel a sensation of coming home to a lost love from a long time ago.
 Also, you will have what I call a glimpse or a peek of who you are in your soul awareness. Something in you will feel the difference in this experience to every other soul mate experience you had on earth. Another reference point are the eyes of your twin as they are truly the windows of the soul, although in this situation this phrase is brought to a whole new level. When you look into your twin's eyes, you are gazing into your own eyes in beauty and amazement. It is as if you dived into this beautiful, warm ocean and you do not ever want to get out. You tend to stare into their eyes and you feel like there are no borders between the two of you.
 Both of your bodies feel each other's energies at the same time and adjust to one another. The ethereal body is the seat of the chakras, the mental body holds the abstract knowledge and concrete

thinking (ego), the physical body is the embodied soul, the astral or emotional body is the storage of our emotions, and the causal body is the seat of the Infinite and soul. All of the bodies contain their own energy and storage and have their own unique function.

When the meeting occurs all of the bodies 'read or scan' the fields of each other for the purpose of remembering. You are given clues all the time for your journey; you are given these deep feelings, which you try to translate. Your DNA starts to decode. We do not see this process with our eyes but certainly, we feel the subtle changes. This is all happening below your conscious awareness and the' reading ' took place when your first meeting happened.

Like all of the big things in life, it started in a precious moment, and this precious moment contained all of the beauty and love for you as a gift. Your DNA started to upgrade and activate. All conscious awakened twin souls are going to operate and function from the *twelve-chakra system* and not seven.

The *seven-chakra system* will become a redundant template as it held the body in a certain vibration at the time we needed this. As the twins move into the twelve-chakra awareness, they vibrate at higher frequencies and experience multidimensionality, meaning that they will embody this cosmic love and work through this love for the higher good of all. It is to this place that humanity is going to evolve slowly in the future.

This precious now moment is all we have, time as we perceive it in this three dimensional space is only a string or continuum of moments which are all contained in one eternal NOW moment.

Feeling the 'lost' love

This meeting will leave you in complete awe, and days after this encounter you will be asking yourself; 'What just happened there? Who is that person? Why do I feel this way? I feel like I have known this person for ages'. That is what your inner dialogue will be like. Your 'ego self' will start to question everything you knew about relationships up to this point because this feeling of instant deep love is something it cannot grasp.

The ego can function in the world only from a stable structure, the ego structure is set in stone, and anything that is a surprise and that causes the ego to experience something different makes it tremble and question a lot.

Your soul is stirred up like a beautiful lake which has been calm for centuries, sleeping a sleep, and now somebody has come along and touched you and said; 'Beloved it is time to wake up, I am here, remember me, remember you'.

Your ego does not like this disturbance, of course. Your ego wants to remain the same as before the meeting happened, in fear, with all of its old beliefs about love and the way love should look and feel. Your ego will go on and on, asking how you can love a person when you don't even 'know' them? How can that even happen? Maybe it is not true? Maybe you invented the whole thing and so on, but at the same time you know in your heart that something profound has happened. Indeed your new life has begun, your life after this meeting will take a completely new direction. The interesting thing is that you do not know it yet.

That is why life is so beautiful and surprising, we truly don't know what the next present moment is going to bring, and even while we are experiencing something sometimes we don't know the full purpose or meaning at the time.

We can only see the tapestry of our lives in retrospect when we look back and connect all the dots. Then we can clearly see why something happened exactly the way it did. Life is a true PRESENT. After you meet your twin soul, you will never be the same again. At the time when you meet them it is good to be aware of the life you have chosen for yourself up to now, even if it is chaotic. When you meet your twin soul you will start to realize that you caused this meeting, it didn't happen by chance, and it is the same in every area of your life. Be aware that you are the creator of everything in your life, and if you think you are not creating, think again, because even if you choose not to change a thing, by not choosing you are still making a choice. We are powerful beyond our wildest dreams and we can use this life power to create anything. This higher power of energy, chi, prana, God/Goddess, Brahman, Tao, source, or whatever you want to call this divine grace has no negative or positive charge until we choose to give one to our creation.

By our conscious awareness and participation, we shape this energy into our creation.

A glimpse of who you are

The meeting happened. You were allowed to have just a glimpse of the paradise you were in and the love that you are. From the ego perspective this love seems so impossible that you try to shut it down every time you feel a deep feeling of love for this person.
 Your thought processes are telling you that it is better not to feel it, than to have it and to lose it again. Somewhere in your

subconscious the knowledge is registered from before that you lost this love or you could not unite into this union.
Even a glimpse was enough to initiate you into this divine journey. Even a glimpse of the nectar of love is enough to last for a lifetime and once you drink from it you will want to return to this feeling many times throughout your life and through many lifetimes.

Searching for the fire in your own soul reflected through the Beloved of your heart, what could be more divine?

This feeling is so beautiful and so intimidating at the same time that you are left confused. Even if we are not aware of so many things consciously, our subconscious communicates with us all the time. It sends us information on a regular basis which we try to block most of the time.
 My personal experience tells me that we are here on earth to connect with that knowledge which we already know, and to resurrect again while in our bodies.
When we die we gain a broader perspective about the life we lived but we don't have to wait until we die to see the truth, we just have to accept and allow the healing rays to wipe out all that is not aligned with truth.
 In the end, all of our experiences finally lead us to our own hearts and the only question we have to ask ourselves is; have I entered my kingdom yet? The other question is; what am I waiting for?

Meditation
Meet your Twin Soul

This meditation came to me during my *Separation Phase* and its purpose is for you to know that your twin is always with you and that you can connect whenever you wish to. The purpose and the intent of this meditation is healing and connecting to your twin soul. It may reassure you to know that you don't need to be physically with your twin to feel their love and support. You will feel that separation is an illusion.

Find some place comfortable where you can sit or lie down in peace, where you will not be interrupted for half an hour. Concentrate on relaxing your body completely and start breathing deeply a couple of times. Close your eyes. Enter your inner space and relax, breathe to let the tension out of the body and be aware of the breath coming in through your nose and going out of your nose. Watch and observe the breath and relax even more deeply.

In your inner eye and your heart vision, start to see yourself walking through a beautiful forest, which leads to a place where you are going to meet your twin. The forest is so calm and beautiful, green and lush, bursting with life, and as you listen to all of the birds singing in tune, you feel the ground beneath your feet, you smell the freshness of the clean air; it is a beautiful warm summer's day. You feel at peace and at one with nature. In this perfect moment, you feel completely at peace and as if nothing is missing.

The sun is warming up your whole body. As you walk in peace and harmony with all that is, a path begins to appear and you notice a small garden space with a bench on it. It looks beautiful with all the surrounding flowers and the little fountain just beside the bench. You sit down and enjoy it, listening to the sound of the birds, the sound of the water, you feel completely at peace.

Now you call your spiritual guide who works with you on this journey to sit with you, and silently say: *Let this meeting of my twin soul bless me and my twin, and everybody involved, for the benefit of all. So be it in unconditional love.*

Your guide is sitting beside you and can call your twin to approach and sit between you on a bench. If your twin appears it is fine, if not you can feel your twin in energy form and have an inner knowledge of them. Feel the love energy. Feel the fullness of this moment. Your twin is in front of you, look at their face, and look deep into their eyes. Feel the energy of this connection. What does it tell you, how do you feel? You can ask them anything you want. Notice all. Listen with all your being for the answers. You can ask your spiritual guide to tell you both something about this connection and give you clarity. You can talk to your guide about your connection as they know both of your hearts. At this moment your heart is the organ of fire, observe this fire in your heart.

Feel your twin's energy and hug them with your own energy. Breathe and relax into this love. Even if you do not see them this time, do not be sad or discouraged as they are always with you. Capture all of these feelings inside of your heart and know your truth. Thank your spiritual guide for supporting you in this journey and being by your side. Anytime you wish you can come and feel this love and drink from its well. Now open your eyes and breathe slowly for a while. Stay in this love during the day. Connect to this union and love so you can be strong when it becomes challenging. The love is always here and your twin supports you all the way.

Invocation
I found you

Oh, flesh of my flesh, heart of my heart,
thank you for the joy of knowing who I am through you.
Thank you for holding the mirror for me so I can see.
I know you, yes, I know you in me, I know me in you.
When our eyes locked, I felt that I existed no more.
Who was I? I was all of existence; I was an ocean of love.
I was the 'I am' in the heart of creation.
'I' was but an illusion lost.
I was in you, bathing in this love.
I knew you forever and finally found you.
Do you remember me, oh my sweetness?
Do you recognize the feeling of coming home,
coming back to your own soul, the eternal one?
Creative, joyful and all loving.
Filled with peace, beauty, and grace.
Filled with love and light.
I found you, I found you
You found me, you found me.
I see you my beloved, I see you,
You are here, at last you are here.

CHAPTER THREE

THE PINK BALLOON PHASE

'You have been with me from the very first life. You are my first memory every time, the single thread in all of my lives. It's you who makes me a person'.

Ann Brashares, My name is memory

"The soul that sees beauty may sometimes walk alone".

Johann Wolfgang von Goethe

Tasting the divine love

After the initial meeting you feel like lightning has struck you, but in a good way. You feel full of energy, and are flying on the wings of love. This feeling of heaven takes over. You are in love and you love this person, and being together feels like coming home after a long pilgrimage. You want to spend all of the time in the world with them and it feels good.

In this phase of your twin soul journey you feel like you have entered the door of heaven and you cannot believe that it opened for you. You see and feel that this is the sensation of love and you realize that this is who you are; it feels like you are complete even if it lasts for a second, a day, or a month. At the same time there is constant talk going on inside your head getting in the way of this love. This chatter is the result of your ego conditioning.

The *Pink Balloon Phase*, as I like to term it, cannot last because at this point in your journey you are still not aware of what is occurring, and probably not ready to hold on to this high vibration of unconditional love. We as humans are individuals with our own wishes, customs, projections, conditioning and years of being taught what and how relationships should be. Now this connection is here in your life to confront you with everything you know about relating to another and this is not easy. You are divided between what you are conditioned to think about love and what you deeply feel in your heart. This pink balloon phase could last forever if we knew how to love and what love truly is. But the whole purpose of this connection is to teach us how to love unconditionally.

Everything we were taught up to that point was conditioned; we as a species haven't got a chance in this society to learn about unconditional love because we have been taught to think about love in a certain way. Through our upbringing, and with popular culture, songs, movies, and media we were shown images of how love should look, and this connection shows us something different.

The whole illusion around love was sold to us as true, but now we are waking up from all of this conditioning about love. We see that it is false and when you meet your twin all preconceptions start to crumble, even about the one love that should be without condition, which is the love of our parents. The love of a parent should be the closest vibration to this unconditional love, but from experience in life we all know that with most who play the role of a parent, this is not so. Everybody who is a parent knows the feeling of loving their child but if we are honest with ourselves we know that only a small percentage of parents give their love freely and without any conditions. From an early age we have been taught that in order to be loved and feel love we must act in a certain way, in other words that we must earn love.

Twin soul journey, teaches us the true meaning of love, it teaches us that love is within us like a never ending stream of energy and that we are worthy of unconditional love no matter what we do.

At this stage of this journey you want to hold on to this relationship so badly that every time you physically separate from your twin it hurts, because twin souls are connected not only through the heart (heart chakra), but also through the 'gut' (the solar plexus), where the power of life force is.

Through my experience I felt this pain in my solar plexus for my twin so many times and, once, when I was crying and calling his name it felt like my gut was like a hollow place that was yearning to be filled up with this peace and love I felt for him. It was something that was calling me towards love. It was very physical, and this was not a mental thing. Every time we separated, I felt like I had literally lost my heart.

Twin souls are connected through all chakras, and this can be very painful if you are not aligned and aware of what is going on between your two energies. Your twin is your magnifying mirror, your ultimate reflection, and you cannot deny what you see when you are in their presence. As time passes by, slowly the descent from heaven starts to happen. This pink balloon phase cannot last at this point in the journey and this 'drop' must happen because we are so deeply conditioned and because this divine love does not accept anything but the truth.

Know that wherever you are in your twin soul journey this Union cannot survive in falsehood.

Slowly it strips away all of the layers of belief, lies, and masks you created to 'protect' your false self and now all this no longer serves you and you are prepared for union and the manifestation of this love on earth.

Shaking of belief systems

When this pink balloon phase starts to burst under the pressure of our beliefs and conditioning, is when the situation gets difficult. You start to see through the illusion of the world around you. You feel this intense love for your twin soul, and at the same time you see that it doesn't work when you try to normalise it or put it in a box.
 You start to project everything you have been conditioned to believe onto your twin soul connection, and try to fit this connection into your former pattern of relating to people, but this does not work. Then the ego clash happens between both twins, and sometimes it seems impossible to grasp the complete intensity of this connection, but know that even when the ego is playing out in the strongest way, your twin will never say something to hurt you. If you are in an abusive relationship and you think this person is your twin, they most likely are not.
In twin soul connection, even in the hardest and darkest moments, there is always respect and deep love for the other.
Your spirit tells you that your twin loves you more than anything and you feel it, but at the same time they act the opposite of how you thought love should feel and look and this gets very confusing. So when this dynamic occurs you cannot understand why it happens and it drives you insane. Both twins are afraid, and act out of fear. It is now that you start to observe the fears of your twin but ironically not your own yet.
 Despite the fact that you love your twin more than anything in the world, you are telling yourself a completely opposite story in your head, all because of fear. Some twin soul couples are only together for a short time as was my own experience, but those few times we were together were enough to last me for a lifetime. The length of time spent together with your twin, or how often you see each other does not matter when applied to this connection. Anything

you do at this stage of your journey that is dictated by your ego, won't help you make sense of this connection. Everything that you thought about love in this connection is turned upside down.

In my personal experience, my twin and I were seeing each other for a period of time but it was never a defined thing, we were not a couple as in 'girlfriend and boyfriend'. From the beginning this 'relationship' had the aura of mystery and uncertainty. We were more to each other than we could ever perceive consciously, but in the three dimensional reality it appeared different. We were meeting on and off, uncertain of anything.

The length of this pink balloon phase is not important, because you must know that when you are in the presence of your twin even a minute can seem like a year of learning and beauty.

The linear timeframe does not apply to twin soul connections and every time you are near your twin you enter another dimension of existence where time ceases to be. Your learning experiences accelerate in the presence of your twin soul even if in terms of linearity your time spent together feels short.

I always felt that I had so little time with my twin, because our meetings always seemed so rushed, our time spent with each other always felt like we came together to work on something and then had to go our separate ways again. Subconsciously I knew this to be true.

It always felt like we were supposed to meet without knowing when we would see each other again and so we would meet, spend some time together, learn something, anchor the love and then separate again. The feeling was as if we could not be together because we would burn from the inside, rather than be nourished from this fire we felt. Now I know we were not ready and we could not possibly compress this connection into the old mould of existing and relating.

Linear time does not apply to this connection because you experience a love so deep that time ceases to exist when you are together. If you and your twin stayed together, you would not learn as much as when you separated. Now I know that separation was needed and that it was divinely orchestrated. You may think that this feeling of time standing still is an effect of every experience of falling in love, but in this connection the cessation of time is not a concept but is experienced first-hand. You literally have a feeling that time does not exist, and nobody else is around you.

When you are in the presence of your twin you enter into such a meditative and blissful state, and it feels so natural.

In this feeling of being at one with the Universe, you get a glimpse into a realm of silence and stillness. It is the mystical experience of a high order. It feels as if you are in the presence of the Divine gazing at you, and showing you who you really are. These mystical moments are a doorway for truly meeting yourself. In this pink balloon love phase, you enjoy this bliss, this gift of love.

You and your twin can be similar in so many things but opposite in expression, meaning that you are different personalities with your own beliefs but in higher reality (the soul) you are one. What one learns the other one learns also, even if it is in a different way. You can actually finish each other's sentences, and when you have a conversation they may use the same sentences and expressions as you. You look into each other's eyes and see no end and no beginning, you see only the infinite ocean that you are.

Your twin is the only person who can awaken you more deeply than anyone else. They will wake you up so you can ascend together. Their words have a powerful energetic charge that resonates differently from other peoples' words. Words you speak to each other can be so powerful that they echo in your inner being long after they are said.

Until perhaps after a long time you awaken to their meaning, and you see the truth. The words my twin wrote to me at the beginning of our connection woke me up completely to the truth of love twenty years later, and when I grasped this in a mystical moment, I knew that we had made a contract together to slowly remember who we are to each other.

The note was as follows:
You are my dark haired, most beautiful, Beloved
Never gotten over of, lifelong eternal angel.

When I saw the complete truth, twenty years later I returned the same message to him and it felt like I had closed the circle of love.
This felt so crazy and magical at the same time. Every time we talked I could hear him saying things that I say to other people in conversations, and in those mystical moments, the feeling was as if I saw myself from an outside perspective, as if I was looking at myself in him. You know how we cannot see ourselves in the mirror as somebody else sees us, yet this time I saw myself through his words, through him.
These mystical moments are so deep that sometimes it is hard to put them into words. That is why none of the regular relationship rules apply to this connection.
Every time that twin souls connect they continue where they left off, no matter how many years have passed in terms of linear time, it always seems like no time has passed, it seems like everything happened yesterday. This is very worrying for our egos because the ego has its own set rules about love and time, and in general, if you don't see somebody for ten years you lose track of how they are, what's been going on in their lives and so on.
In this connection, you do not need any three-dimensional facts; you just know how your twin is and feels. You see through all of the illusion that was presented about love.

For example, if you see a soul mate ex-boyfriend after a long time you are going to be aware that time has passed between you and feel a need to ask them what is going on, how are they and so on, but when you meet your twin, even if it is after twenty years, you will feel this instant connection.

You will feel like you saw them yesterday and just continue where you left off. This feeling is so real that it wakes you up to the realisation that there is something bigger going on. To the ego, it is impossible to be connected to somebody when you haven't seen them for a while, because ego functions on a local level and is based only on this earth reality, while our soul is non-local, meaning it is universal and can experience simultaneously whatever it wishes for.

In my experience of this connection, whenever I met with my twin it was magnificent and beautiful; we did not have much time together, but even the shortest of times were eternal. I always felt this love in my spirit but my ego was persuading me that love should look and appear in a certain way. We were both very young when we met; I was seventeen, and he was twenty.

I felt this love from the beginning and he did too, but on the conscious level he tried to suppress it and run from this connection, so that I ended up being the 'chaser' and he took the role of the 'runner'. Bear in mind that the 'runner' and 'chaser' are only concepts for easier understanding, because in this connection, both twins end up being chasers and runners but each plays one role more actively.

Both twins will at some point be runners and chasers, it cannot be otherwise because they are balancing each other from the inside. My twin and I have set ourselves the hard task of not even being physically together all the while having long periods of separation.

You must be aware that some twin 'relationships' are never sexually consummated and if this is your experience, then know that this is ok. This happens not because they don't want to experience sexuality together but because this is such a deep soul love that sometimes it feels as if you would ruin its perfection if you have the 'common' 3D sex. However if it happens it is ok.

If you are experiencing this soul connection you will always feel that with your twin it would not be a regular sexual experience but rather the union of soul and body. You feel that aura of sacredness around when you think of making love to your twin. Even if you didn't sexually merge here in 3D you will often experience astral sex with your twin and see that you are already merged in your soul. These experiences will always feel sacred and beautiful.

In my experience I wanted all of my innocence to belong to him and when we couldn't stay together I rejected him.

I always felt the sacredness of this connection, though this is not to say that other soul mate relationships are not sacred, but in my heart, I knew that he was the one for me. That my body belonged to him and his body was made for me like a special design from the divine.

We as humans are among the only species on earth who do not have sex merely for the survival of the species. Other species mate for the sole reason of keeping their species alive. As humans we should be conscious of what sexual intimacy can give and take at the same time, if we are practising it unconsciously. Even at a young age I felt this to be true, and was conscious about the power of sexual relations all along the way.

Every partner we have leaves an imprint of their energy in our auric field. You create a soul tie with any person with whom you are sexually intimate and if you are not completely conscious, you can drain yourself of your own energy.

When you become aware of this sacred bond between you and your twin, you keep your body and soul 'pure' for them, but however, there are no fixed rules because the separation can last long in many cases and that does not mean that you have to live in celibacy until you reunite again. Your twin soul connection does not preclude you from exploring relationships with other soul mates and having rich experiences in your life.

I am not trying to advise people not to engage in sexual relationships, but rather to become conscious of your sexual relations and of who and why you 'give' your body, because every sexual encounter is much more than the physical and at the same time it is a strong energy exchange. In your twin soul journey you will have a period of complete lack of sexual desire. This is caused by the balancing of the ascension energies in your body.
You won't have any desire even if the 'sexiest' body is displayed in front of you, if it is not aligned with soul desire. In a way you will not be interested in anyone else except your twin. You just can't relate to the former ways of sexual expression any more. This lack of sexual desire won't bother you at all because you will see clearly now that it has a higher purpose, and that is to clear you of all the old ways of expressing your sexuality. You will clearly see after this process passes that the soul is fully in charge.

Now as conscious humans, we should know that sexual connections are more than pleasure, with the right person they can be the entrance to heavenly realms.

Always know that each twin relationship is specific, and the patterns of each twin soul journey manifest themselves differently.

This is a list of negative beliefs you might have about true unconditional love that may be holding you back from achieving union with your beloved twin soul.
Be aware that perhaps you don't even know that you have some of these beliefs, so you may have to really 'dig' deep into yourself to see which ones you hold, to be able to change each one of them so you can come into Union with your Beloved.

- ❖ *I don't deserve this beautiful unconditional love.*
- ❖ *I am not 'this lucky'.*
- ❖ *My twin soul cannot love me unconditionally.*

- *I cannot love unconditionally.*
- *Being in a relationship is always subject to conditions.*
- *My twin cannot love me for who I truly am.*
- *My twin would not love me unconditionally if they truly saw me.*
- *This kind of love exists only in fairy tales.*
- *This deep soul love is a myth.*
- *If I surrender to this love I might become vulnerable.*
- *Even if this love is true I will lose it at some point.*
- *I am separate from my twin soul.*
- *I am undeserving of true love.*
- *I think 'true love' doesn't exist.*
- *I don't believe in love.*
- *This soul love feels like a 'dream come true' and I don't believe in dreams.*
- *If I surrender to this love I am going to lose 'myself'.*
- *I am not strong enough to endure the obstacles in this twin soul Union.*
- *If I come into Union with my twin my family will reject me.*

The opposite of these negative beliefs are:

- *I deserve this beautiful unconditional love.*
- *I am the 'luckiest' person and my soul wished for this experience of meeting my twin soul.*
- *My twin soul loves me unconditionally.*
- *I can love my twin soul unconditionally.*
- *Being in a relationship with my twin soul is unconditional.*
- *My twin loves me for who I truly am.*
- *My twin truly sees me and loves me unconditionally no matter what.*
- *This soul love exists and is true.*

- ❖ *This deep soul love is the reality of my experience.*
- ❖ *When I surrender to this love I feel true intimacy.*
- ❖ *True love cannot be 'lost'.*
- ❖ *I am already one with my twin soul.*
- ❖ *I deserve to be loved unconditionally and experience true love.*
- ❖ *True love exists, it is real and alive.*
- ❖ *I believe in love.*
- ❖ *I believe that dreams come true and this love is one of my dreams.*
- ❖ *If I surrender to this love I will gain my true self.*
- ❖ *I am strong enough to endure any obstacle in the way of this twin soul Union.*
- ❖ *When I come into Union with my twin my family will see the power of true love.*

Putting the love into a box and healing your inner child

Subconsciously, both twins feel that this is the very heart of the sacred connection in every way. This love is true, so true that it makes you question the reality in which you were incarnated. This love does not need physical closeness, it does not know about the passing of time as we perceive it.

As my twin and I were meeting on and off during a period of a few years, whenever we met it felt like no time had passed in between, it always felt intimate and beautiful.

True twin flame or twin soul experience is hardest at the beginning when you are not so conscious of what is happening and it is surely not for the faint of heart. Nobody in their right mind would wish it upon themselves consciously.

The twin soul journey is not easy and those souls who want to master themselves chose this experience before birth.

During my exploration of the experiences of many twins, and through soul mate relationship coaching, I could never fully understand the desire that people have to be in this kind of connection because this connection is not a game, it is hard work and can be a very maddening experience. When you are in the midst of this madness of in-between realities, you start to question even your own sanity and that is no walk in the park. In moments of doubt you have to trust your connection and your heart to the utmost and this is very difficult. You have to be willing to jump into the unknown, trust that if you have the desire for its fulfilment, this fulfilment is on the way to you because the desire would not exist otherwise.

God doesn't ever put a desire in your heart without giving you the way to fulfilling it.

This connection tests you to the bones and to your core beliefs. It shakes your beliefs about love, children, marriage, relationships, the world, parenting, and your mission in life.

This connection is an earthquake for the ego, and in the end, the ego has to surrender in the name of love. This connection is the hardest and at the same time the most beautiful experience. It opens up wounds and shadow parts of yourself that you have buried deeply and that you did not know even existed.

This is why, through my experience of this union, I know that there are no runners and chasers. By blaming your twin for not loving you, or by asking yourself why they are running, or expecting them to act in a certain way, you are running simultaneously and not aware of it. You are running from yourself, from looking deeply into your own being. You are projecting so much of the unconscious onto your twin.

You are afraid of your subconscious mind, and of what you might find there, so it is easier to project everything onto your twin and point the finger. So many twins along the way think that one is more evolved than the other, and that is the illusion, because your twin does not have to learn his lessons the same way you do, and he or she does not have to appear 'spiritual' at all to be able to integrate within themselves. The process of ascension is doing its job whether you are willing to participate or not.

The indicator of how well you are surrendering to the process of ascension is the pain; if you are in pain be aware that you are resisting the healing and the possibility of letting go.

If you contact your twin on a false premise or if you have not started to look within, they will reject you and this is only an outer reflection of what is going on inside of you. They are a mirror. When you reject yourself they reject you.

Your twin knows and feels you, and they cannot let anything false be within you, even if that means rejecting you. Twin soul love is that kind of love.

At this point of diving deep and working on yourself, your inner child wakes up for attention, and so I am now going to say something about this subject. It is very essential to work on healing your inner child. Your inner child is your unattended and wounded self from birth until you were a child of approximately seven years old. By that time all of our subconscious beliefs are formed and the core belief of how we perceive the world in general, as a safe or dangerous place. Your inner child is your innocence that wants to be recognized and acknowledged, because be assured that no matter what anybody did to you or said to you in your childhood they could not touch the God-like essence of you, ever. This essence in you stays as pure as it was on the day you were born, and that God-like essence is pure love.

You will have to heal your wounded child but be aware of that divine part of you that is untouched.

Your inner child wants your attention, your communication and you have to see and acknowledge it. You must be a true parent to your beautiful inner child. You can listen to this inner child, make it confident, and nourish it now that you are an adult.
Childhood is over but your inner child is always alive and present. I don't know who said it but you know the saying; 'It is never too late to have a happy childhood'. All of us have been raised to believe that when we enter adulthood, this child is lost. In this way we suppressed the child in us, and for a long time believed that this child was gone. The inner child is our inner genius, and as we remember our inner child and our innocence, this genius can fully awaken for true miracles to happen.

In each one of us lives a seven year old who is still innocent, beautiful, curious, playful, smart, intelligent, intuitive, and full of wonder and magic, and no matter where you come from, what you look like and believe, it is there inside of you.

It is alive and waiting to communicate with us. What happened to us in the meantime and when did we kill our innocence? The lack of this knowledge is why we walk around like zombies asking ourselves; what is my purpose, what do I like to do?
When we were children we never had to ask those questions, we knew what to do. We soared into love and creativity from moment to moment and expressed ourselves through play. Why should now, when we are adults, be any different? We should be able to express, fly, and put our God-given talents to use. I believe everybody has a natural born talent, it is just a matter of whether

they explored it and decided to be brave and put it to use. Why do we stuff our inner child with 'unhealthy' food, television, people who drain our energy, hideous tight clothes, and things our child does not want to do, when all it wants is to be free and playful?

Our inner child more than anything wants to be free to play and create.

During most of our adult life we 'shut down' and distract our inner child. We distract ourselves with food, shopping, television, clubbing, drinking, but these are only temporary escape routes because we all know we cannot escape ourselves. In this society we are taught to anesthetize and numb our feelings instead of acknowledging and processing them.
When you start to awaken to the truth these escapes won't comfort you anymore.

Only a person lacking spiritual awareness can sedate and numb their feelings. To be able to wake up, we have to feel our pain, and come to the other side where love is.

We have cut this precious bond between our adult-self and our-child self and pretend that we are over it. It so important to address this issue, and in my opinion when we all return to that innocence, the world will know peace. Have you ever had an experience of looking at people and whilst interacting with them, in a split second, you see their inner child on their faces? In my soul journey of awakening there was a period when I encountered this all of the time. I saw a 'small 'version of them in the physical form whilst talking to them. Sometimes it would be very funny when I had encounters with people who tend to be 'serious' adults.
They would adopt a pose and act in a certain way, completely hardened by the layers of their ego protection, and then their inner child would pop up and energetically tell me the funniest thing.

Their inner child would tell me what they liked to do, what their dreams were, or the 'child' would make a funny gesture. When I would tell people what their inner child was doing, they would usually cry in recognition. It was at this time that I experienced the realisation that we are not grown-ups. We adopted the term 'grown-up' to mean adult and mature but a grown-up is only layers and layers of conditioning and bad advice. Nothing is ours. Then I saw the spiritual truth of us humans.

In the heart of our heart, we are all good, and we all want to be loved and caressed, we want to be validated and embraced. At the heart of every wish of our human experience, there is a desire to be loved and acknowledged. To be truly seen.

The only difference between us humans is how badly we each have been conditioned to believe we are not worthy and loved enough to live a life of abundance and joy, which is our birthright. This is the reason that I don't believe in organized religions, because of the way they divide more than they unite.

They accentuate the differences rather than reinforce the similarities between humans. If you are a follower of an organized religion my advice to you is take the good parts from the teaching but always think with your own head, and above all take in only what resonates with your own inner being. Be intelligent.

I personally believe in one love, which originates from one source for the whole of humanity. When you start to communicate with your inner child, it can seem very overwhelming, because we are not educated in society to talk to the inner recesses of our being. In this society, you know where people end up who talk to themselves. We have been numbed and disconnected from our inner beings for so long but if you listen, your inner child will tell you what it wants, what hurts him/her, what are his/her dreams.

When you start healing this aspect of yourself, you will meet yourself in a completely new light. You can be mad, hurt or even refuse to talk to your inner child for making such demands on you, and your child can be mad at you as well, but slowly you can come to loving terms with each other. Now you are the conscious adult and can embrace that wounded child completely and give it unconditional love. We are all this innocent seven year old who is playing for a while on this planet.

When people carry so much pain inside of them, if the pain is not brought to the surface of the conscious mind it turns to aggressiveness, destructiveness, and a tendency to hurt others. This happens because we haven't learnt to love ourselves.

When you look at people you interact with daily just ask yourself; how can I be mad at a seven year old? Try it and you will see that the energy will immediately shift. Whenever you are mad or unforgiving to yourself or someone else, imagine this child standing in front of you. It is impossible to stay mad because the image of their inner child will soften your heart and bring compassion. Many people are stuck psychologically at this age because of their unresolved wounding from their childhood so when interacting with people they react from that wounded inner child.

All of our core wounds and imprints are caused in childhood by our parents, caretakers, and society and everything else is just learned and appended on top of that. All that we added on our life journey, which we call knowledge, is pale in comparison to the insights of the heart, the riches of our soul.

The true knowledge is stored inside the chambers of your soul and nothing can destroy or touch it; all the gold we search for is hidden inside of us. In this innocence deep inside we know everything, we just have to remember and bring our innocence out to shine. This knowing does not come instantly but as you go forward and progress on your spiritual journey, it ripens inside of you until it is ready.

As you mature on your spiritual journey, you begin to 'download' a different kind of knowledge from a universal library. Your imagination is enhanced and your inner senses sharpen.

Everything in nature has its time of growth and its time of being still, and if you pick a premature fruit before time, it will not give you the sweetness of ripeness.
Patience is the core of all spiritual growth; we can ruin something if we lack patience and then we need to start all over again, whereas if we waited just a little bit longer the understanding would come. I love the word 'patience'. The twin soul journey among other things teaches you patience. It teaches you to flow with the divine will and synchronize yourself with this flow. It teaches you to wait for the right moment in everything. As soon as you step out of your ego identification this flow will take over because there are no more obstacles. This patience prepares you to be ripe for the gift of love, so you can enjoy it fully in awareness. It teaches you the patience of knowing the divine timing in life. It teaches you to be ready to receive with gratitude and love.
 We humans tend to complicate so many things, but if we stop and observe nature and how nature behaves we would see that we are no different. Nature goes in cycles, and each cycle is interwoven with another cycle. All cycles are equally important. The seasons change in complete harmony with all of life, we are of this nature and in understanding nature, we can understand ourselves. Our bodies are made of cycles and contain seasons. The moon affects the tides in the same way it affects us. We just have to have patience and observe.
On a twin soul journey you are going to be talking a lot with your inner child, surrendering everything you thought you knew, and you will be quoting this famous conclusion of Socrates a lot.
The Socratic paradox is; *'I know that I know nothing'* and accepting that will be the beginning of a new emergence of heart

wisdom. This will be the beginning of surrender. You will be pushed to empty your mind more than once; keep it empty and be ready to fill it up with nothing but love. You are going to try to put this love into a box, a nice little box with all of the prettiest ribbons and colours. You are going to try to make sense of this connection, but the harder you try the crazier it gets.

The day will come when you are left there open and vulnerable, for a new understanding to come and you will know something beautiful has occurred. You are ready for the teachings of your heart.

Maybe for the first time a true prayer is going to come out of your heart and you are going to hear what your soul wisdom is trying to tell you.

You will know that a prayer is a surrender to the will of the Divine, through your vulnerability. You are going to welcome the genuine prayer, a cry from your inner being for the explosion of the Divine within you.

In this mystical moment you are going to admit to yourself that you love your twin and that this love is never going to disappear. In this moment of surrender you are truly going to accept this sacred love.

A glimpse of heaven

In this pink balloon phase, whenever you are in the presence of your twin soul you feel so connected to life, so safe, that it feels like you just landed on the softest cloud and all the angels are singing the most beautiful hymns of love just for the two of you.

It is natural that you want to hold on to this beautiful feeling, you are just now remembering your united consciousness, your completeness as a soul.

But in this phase, you are not ready yet for the force of this love. You are allowed to just catch a glimpse of heaven, a peek into this paradise and just a taste of this unconditional love. This force of God-like intelligence is very wise and all seeing. There is nothing we can do from our human perspective to force anything in this sacred connection. We begin to realise that nothing is under our control and that divine timing is at work all of the time in this connection.

Everything comes to us when we need it for our highest growth and not a minute before or after. This is trust and surrender. The act of complete trust is called 'faith'.

When you have faith, you know that the whole serves you and you serve the whole for the best of all purposes. This connection is under a Divine protection. The feeling of heaven can manifest in so many ways, but one of the most common experiences is the ceasing of time and the receding of the world around us.

When you are around your twin soul you cannot have the feeling of time passing in a conventional way, because you get lost in a timeless world and that is the dimension where love exists. Love does not exist in time but rather in a zero point awareness of the present and your twin is the only one who can orbit you there.

Zero point awareness for me exists in each now moment we are given. If you are projecting into the past or the future, you are missing the knowing, missing the love.

The next thing you may experience is a feeling of simultaneous aloneness and togetherness, as if all of existence disappears during this time whilst gathering in one spot just for the two of you. In these mystical moments you feel supremely connected, significant, and existentially validated. You feel truly alive. You feel so purely creative in these moments. This is why I call this phase a pink balloon, in which you want to stay forever. It is a glimpse into forever and into the eternal point of yourself immersed in love.

You feel like anything is possible with your twin. You come in and out of this phase. It goes on until all of your different beliefs clash between your two worlds, because even if this is your twin he or she was conditioned and programmed differently from you. Since you cannot fit the relationship into any box, you give up for the moment and you think to yourself that it is over between you.

This is only your ego projection because later in the journey you realize that it is far from over, in fact it is just the beginning. The ego functioning is very deceitful, telling you lies, but this love is so powerful that no lie can conquer it. That is why the ego has to be so 'strong' because otherwise how would it help you see the ingenuity of transforming you into a being full of love?

Meditation
Knowing and loving your inner child

The purpose of this meditation is healing your inner child. For you to be able to come into union, you have to be willing to balance yourself through talking to your inner child, recognizing your trauma, and the ways you have been wounded.
It is a beautiful way of connecting to yourself and healing. It is beautiful and freeing to truly accept and see your inner child and your innocence.

Sit or lie down somewhere comfortable and in peace for half an hour. Breathe deeply a few times and notice the breath coming in and out of your body. You feel alive with every breath. Relax completely and feel your body touching the bed or the place on which you are sitting. Take a few deep breaths and close your eyes.
See in your inner eye and vision a beautiful sunny day, it is autumn. Notice the leaves that cover the ground, all the beautiful colours of the fall. Orange, brown and ruby red are the hues of the magnificent trees; hear the sound of the leaves under your feet as you walk. See the beauty and the richness of the season. You walk and you feel completely at peace and relaxed, you see in the distance a magnificent building that looks like a hotel and you approach it. As you enter you see an elevator and press the basement button, all along the way you feel safe and secure. When you come out of the elevator, you see a theatre with red seats and a stage. It feels warm and cosy. You choose a seat and relax. You will be the observer of your inner child. On stage, there is your inner child when you were seven years old. You observe the child, how does the child feel, how is it dressed; you can ask him/her questions. You can ask your inner child whatever you want.
Now reach out to this child and tell him/her that you love them and that they are safe. Ask him/her to come and join you on your

seat, look them in the eyes and hug them. Say aloud; 'I am here for you now and I love you'. Give the love to your inner child. You can then call forth your inner child aged fourteen, and your adolescent self at twenty-one so that every seven year stage is covered.

You can also call your inner child at any age you feel your inner child needed attention, protection and love. You hug and love your inner child and tell him/her that from now on you are here for him/her. Observe this child and be with them. Feel any emotion that comes up, validate their feelings and embrace the child. Be with them for some time and do not rush the process.

Feel this healing meditation in your heart. Whatever emotions come up accept them, your emotions will guide you on your healing journey. When you are ready open your eyes, and know that you are a true parent to your inner child and that you are healing right now. You are whole and enough.

Invocation
Sacred love

Through this sacred love I recognize myself and who I am,
through this love I see the truth hidden behind the veil.
So many veils, were covering my beauty.
In this love I swim into the ocean of my depth,
in this love I am my true self,
In this love I see my beauty and my divinity.
Through this love, I embrace all,
I see all as a reflection of my heart,
I see clearly that I am all and that all is myself.
There was never separation, only unity.
In this love, I am alive, so alive.
I am in love.

CHAPTER FOUR

THE SEPARATION
-The runner chaser dynamic-

'The reason it hurts so much to separate is because our souls are connected'.

Nicholas Sparks

"I faced it all, and I stood tall, and did it my way".

Frank Sinatra

Missing the love

At this stage of the journey you have decided to separate from each other. Even if you thought otherwise from the physical perspective and your ego wanted to hold on to this 'relationship', on a soul level you made an implicit arrangement to go your separate ways for a while.

The separation can last for years or decades, and for how many years all depends on what decisions you have made together with your twin, and you only become aware of this further into the journey. When the separation happens you feel soul pain. This pain occurs because of the rejection of your own soul, and it feels like somebody has stabbed you in the centre of your being, ripped your soul out and threw it in the garbage.

I am describing this soul pain metaphorically in such a strong way for it is the only way I can give a graphic image of the intensity of the pain in order to bring understanding and compassion closer to you.

The pain is strong and can be very physical, meaning that your heart can literally ache as can your stomach where the *third chakra* is located, the place where you and your twin are connected.

You are going to miss the heaven of this connection while at the same time suffering greatly. I would describe this feeling as if God/Goddess took you to see heaven and then kicked you out and said that you cannot stay there because it is not time yet. You are going to feel so alone and abandoned. At this time all of the fears of abandonment will start to surge into your awareness so that you can face and acknowledge them.

When the separation happens, the chasing and running starts, and if it is the case that you are the chaser, you are going to put your life on hold and wait until you get really tired of it. You do not consciously recognise yet that this person is your twin soul but you know that something different and crazy is happening, something you never felt before. It is an unknown feeling and it is scary.

You know in your heart that a love and recognition so perfect cannot be broken and you cling to it as if your life depends on it, and in a way it does. You know subconsciously that certainly your soul growth and union with your twin soul does.

The soul pain

As I have explained, looking at it from a three dimensional perspective, one person takes the role of the chaser and the other the role of the runner. This is how this dynamic looks from the outside, but don't be fooled by the concepts, because such roles do not exist in higher dimensional reality.

In the fifth dimensional reality of perceiving life, you are already with your twin in union for eternity. On the inside something profound is happening; the battle between the ego and soul is starting.

The battle between sense and sensibility is a balancing act. One of you is actively going to take on the role of the chaser and pursue the other one, while the other is going to appear to be running. The chasing and running happens on the outside until you understand that primarily this is an inside dynamic. To chase from the inside means you are trying to keep the control of how, when, and why in the connection. To run from the inside is to suppress your fears and deny the connection . You have to let go of all expectations and surrender completely to the divine will.

The chaser is usually the female because they are more in tune with their emotions but as I always say, every twin soul connection is different so there are no set rules. Even if the feminine tends to recognize these feelings before the masculine, it is always interesting to see the male perspective in this connection, since they can be aware of something that the female is not.

Men have the ability to experience very deep feelings and a huge capacity to love unconditionally. The only difference between masculine and feminine is that the masculine has been more conditioned to keep their feelings bottled up inside for the sake of appearing strong and manly. In a way, men can love even more deeply for the very reasons that I have just mentioned.

Even if your twin appears to be running he/she might be aware of so many things that maybe you are not cognisant of. You are one soul learning from two bodies, learning from two perspectives, from two points of the same view, so according to that premise, one cannot be aware and the other one completely asleep. You follow each other's growth, even if it seems that one twin is more awakened than the other. You are always one with your twin in higher dimensional realities and working on your mission and ascension. From the inside both twins run concurrently, but of course, you do not know that at this stage. You blame and project negative thoughts onto your twin because it is easier for you not to face yourself at this moment.

> *Twins could not complete their healing, introspection and clearing of karmic ties with other soul mates while having the overwhelming presence of their twin beside them, and this is why separation is needed.*

Usually when they meet, they are completely unaware of what is truly going on and they are most definitely not ready for the intensity of this union. Inner conflicts, dilemmas, past conditioning, fears, and insecurities are the reasons why they 'run' from this intense love. It all comes down to how worthy we feel of being loved so deeply and unconditionally. Even in separation twins come back to each other periodically to check up on the progress their twin has made. Your twin wants to extract the best possible version of yourself out of you. This is how much they love you. They see through your efforts to 'beg' for love at the same time knowing that you haven't yet mastered self-love. They see all of you because they are you and this is why the rejection happens with both twins, because of non-acceptance of self. However, my lovely ones, on this journey patience is essential. Patience is faith in action and all is going to be revealed to you in time. Not a moment too soon, and that is the glory and beauty of this journey. Consciousness opens up to you like a long hidden secret of beauty and it removes its veils one by one until you see clearly who you really are.

Divinity is very intelligent and not a thing happens without a reason. You are going to cry a lot in this phase; you are going to be purged and come face to face with your dark or shadow self. As we ascend, we always get the right amount of insight needed for each moment.

You always know what you need to know, in the moment you need to know it.

Do not hold on to outdated concepts and the names we give to this connection, we have to put into language what is divine, and that is not easy sometimes, but we should not hold on to past terminology, even in our innermost selves. We need language only as a road map and not as ultimate truth, because the truth, your truth, is a journey into your own soul and only you can identify what you know to be true for you. We have to call this connection something, we have to name these ethereal and divine feelings, but in the end, you have to dive deep in to your own ocean and find your truth and your heart.

Along my journey, I was questioning myself constantly; 'Is this true? Am I inventing all this? Am I crazy and obsessive over this?'. The best two questions that helped me were; 'is there a soul connection or not between me and this person? Do I feel the magnetic pull towards them?'

Either there is a soul connection or not, there is no confusion there. Either there is a pull or not, no confusion there also. You are connected to your twin in the deepest possible way, so trust what you know in your soul. While this chasing is going on you do not feel so good because it feels like you are trying to hold on to something that does not want to be 'yours'.

However, you must stop and think for a moment why this is so. You are going to think to yourself; 'this love felt so real, why was it taken away from me? How can this love feel so real and yet I cannot be with this person?'This love is so very tangible but since you are not conscious yet of this new fifth dimensional reality, you are going to be fooled a great deal by your ego.

In your ego's consciousness you will think that you are crazy, that a love like this does not exist, that you are needy, that you are probably obsessed, and all kinds of feelings that are not very pleasant, to say the least.

Your ego is going to torture you so it can keep you from this divine love.

I want you to think about this; you cannot be crazy and conscious that you are crazy at the same time. Somebody who is 'crazy' does not know that they are out of touch with reality.

You need awareness and alertness to see your own state of being.

Your internal mind's dialogue is going to be totally against this love, but your heart does not want to give up on this love. Your heart knows what it feels.

The heart intelligence knows what the ego mind cannot possibly ever know.

Your ego cannot know love because it exists only to be our false self in this world, and to serve us in everyday life. Somehow, we lost our way in between journeys and believed our ego to be true. During the separation phase the dissection of the ego starts and you start questioning things a lot. You will be asking so many questions inside of you, but you have no answers yet, and you realize that the question itself is the point sometimes and not the answer. Your life goes on, you live, you laugh, you cry, but you do not forget your twin, you just learn to live without them. You start to compare your previous and later relationships with this connection but with no success. Slowly you start to see that maybe not everything is what it seems in this world, and that things may be far from what they appear to be.

Failure occurs in your logical thinking because your ego is still running the show. You do not know it yet but it is still not time for you to know the full picture. Everything you need to know you will be shown to you when you need to know it, not a moment before, not a moment later. Trust that.

Trust that life always works for your benefit and your highest potential, even when negativity from your ego perspective makes you think otherwise.

We came into this *duality* here on earth and we must be aware that our divinity is not far from us at any moment. We were never separate from God/Goddess or the Divine. On this journey as you surrender and acknowledge the Divine intelligence and its power over your egotistical self, your ego is going to put up a fight. It is going to be a very painful fight, but at the same time very liberating. You did not think that you could become a beautiful butterfly without some pain did you?

Don't explain yourself

This twin soul connection is the most profound experience of your soul. It is firstly an inner soul journey. Be prepared for the reality that most people who do not have this experience will not understand you. We all live in the parallel universes of our own subjective truths and you must not be disappointed if most people do not understand what you are going through.

Everything we go through is experienced from a subjective viewpoint, and it is only when we agree collectively about something, that it becomes a general truth, although there is no such truth as one truth for all. Even if you were the only one in the world feeling these feelings it would not make this experience less valid and true.

All throughout this twin soul journey you will feel alone, abandoned, misunderstood, but you must hold on to what your heart knows to be true. There is nothing easy in following your path of truth and bravery.

Society has taught us the completely opposite lesson which was to follow the crowd in order to feel safe and accepted. This way is the reverse way, the way less walked, and I call it the way of the heart.

The royal walk, the walk of kings and queens, meaning that it is very powerful and sacred. When you speak to someone close to you about this connection, in the majority of cases people will think that you have a huge crush on your ex, they will tell you it is unrequited love, and they will advise you to forget about them. Some will think that you are obsessed or crazy, some will tell you that you deserve better, and so on. Despite all of this, something in you knows your truth, your inner calling. Every heart is called for something, where is your heart calling you?

This connection is you reflected through another soul, another human being and you cannot possibly escape yourself, when you see it clearly mirrored through another.

On this journey you will try everything to erase this connection from your experience, but however hard you try it won't go away. It is like a shadow, metaphorically speaking, so where can you go, where can you escape your shadow? You have additional version of the same you in another body, on this earth experiencing life. When you have this realization, one among many, it is not easy to accept. I know it is not easy, and I feel for you dear friends who are on this twin soul journey, I am aware of your suffering.

At this time, the ego is still not recognized for what it is, and there is still a lot of identification with the ego in this phase. It is all good, as long as we pray for guidance to see our ego for what it is rather than what we think it is.

The ego should be in the service of our hearts and not the other way around. As Einstein wisely said; *"The intuitive mind is a sacred gift and the rational mind is a faithful servant. We have created a society that honours the servant, and has forgotten the gift".*

It is definitely time for us to see this truth clearly.

Dissection of the ego

What does it mean to dissect the ego? It means to observe it so closely and vigilantly that you see how it operates within you. We don't try to get rid of it or try to suppress it, all we need to do is observe and understand the mechanism with which it operates. When we are existing in our ego or our lower self, we suffer.
Suffering shows us that we are not in alignment with our highest truth. On the other hand, the suffering shows us that we do not allow the love to enter our hearts.

We do not need to search for love, we just need to get rid of the layers of lies covering it and allow the love to pour from our being.

When you suffer enough you start to dissect your own ego and question everything about life. It is in the suffering that the shell of the ego starts to break.

Ego is our false self, created by our Divine expression, only for this earthly dimensional reality.

As we play this role perfectly, we forget along the way who we truly are. Ego is only one aspect of our multidimensional Divine self, not the only one as we are conditioned to believe.
When you start to awaken you begin to see patterns in historical events, you see deep into the structures we created in this society that blocked us from our hearts. You start to see the patterns that

run through your lineage, you see the patterns that repeat themselves in your close family and you become aware of the themes that you need to break free from. You see the patterns in the educational system, in the healthcare system; your veils start to fall one at a time.

You start to see your own beliefs about marriage, money, beliefs about love and trust. In general, you see yourself and the world in a new light. You realise that as a twin soul, you are a volunteer soul who came here on earth to help; you firstly help to elevate the unconditional love in everybody who meets you, and secondly, you help to cleanse the pattern or template in the lineage of your blood relatives, your closest family.

It feels like you are standing at the border of the old and new, holding your ancestral baggage, ready to cross over to a new land, and thank them for all that they did. You want to ditch this baggage so you can enter lightly into the new. You are here to conclude the karmic cycles that run in your family and to help create a new way of relating and behaving with each other.

From an early age, many of you felt like peacekeepers in your family, telling them all the time that only love would heal them. You are aware by now of the repetitive behaviour of your ego, and the game of illusion and you start to see more deeply into the functioning of the ego and you begin to understand. You start to lay the foundations of your own reality and realise that it does not have to adhere to the way of your conditioning. You start to see that you can make a new way, your own way. You have a glimpse of the fact that this soul love changes everything, and you see the living truth of what love is.

Love is not some nice romantic word or notion but a living life force energy that can transform and heal everything.

Love is energy, a live stream flowing through us. Only love can give you a new life. Love burns everything that doesn't vibrate in love's frequency. This is why we call this connection twin flame, because it yearns to burn everything on the way to the Divine, it wants to know only love itself. It wants to know the true self. So my question to you is; 'would you 'return' to your twin soul as a beggar or as a queen/king?'

> Until we stop begging for love and see that we are love, we are not in union with self.

Now you know that to be able to come into union, you need to act as a king or queen in your own inner kingdom.

Meditation
Cutting cords for clearing the way to union

The purpose of this meditation is clearing the way for your union by cutting cords with soul mates and whomever you are still attached to in a negative way. These attachments to soul mates you have encountered in your life can slow down your coming into union.

You may also have cords still attached from parents, siblings, friends, and previous partners. These are energy cords and can interfere with your union. In this meditation together with your twin, you are going to clear the way so you can emerge lighter and come into union.

Find a place where you will not be disturbed for a while and where you can relax, sitting or lying down, however you feel more comfortable. Begin by closing your eyes and start to breathe deeply a few times observing the breath coming in and out of your nose. Be aware of your body and feel it. Feel your body touching the surface, the outlines of your body filling a space of the room. You are calm, safe, and relaxed. Watch the breath flow in and out.

See in your inner eye and vision a bridge and the beautiful, magnificent nature surrounding it as you are standing there breathing in the sweetness of this scene. You are grounded and touching the soft grass, feeling completely calm and facing the bridge. Your body feels lighter than air and you are aware of everything around you, the sounds, the smells, and the warmth of the sun. While you stand there, see your beloved beside you giving you strength and love. You smile at each other. Your twin gives you the most magnificent smile.

Now in front of yourself standing on the bridge, see anyone with whom you still have any negative attachments. It might be your parents, ex-partners, siblings or friends past and present.

Now imagine this cord connecting from your solar plexus to theirs, and as you see this ask Archangel Michael to cut the cord with his powerful sword. Now see them crossing that bridge and going away from you. Imagine a big beautiful pink bubble of love and see them enter it. You can do this process with as many people as you need. You can see your twin doing the same with their soul mates. When the cord is cut, ask Archangel Michael to surround you and your twin with his beautiful, magnificent blue light of protection and love. You feel this love bathing every cell of your body. This healing cleanses the old stagnant and possessive energy from your energy field and enables new fresh energy to travel throughout your body. Feel this burst of energy bathing you inside, feel the freshness and lightness in you.

Give thanks to Archangel Michael for this healing. When you think it is time enough, hug your twin, stay in this embrace, and feel the openness of your heart to receive this love and healing whenever you need it. Say this aloud; *'through cutting cords with whomever was hindering my union I release anybody who does not resonate with my highest good, in peace and love. I release myself in unconditional love. My energy is free from old attachments and free to flow towards my sacred union'*. Know that this healing is always available to you. Breathe and let go. It is magical. Thank your twin for sharing this with you and for being here for you. Thank you, thank you, and thank you. May all be blessed.

Invocation
In each other all along

Separated from ourselves
we could not find each other.
Running around like two lost children,
in the search for love.
Chasing each other through eternity.
Yearning to be found, separated again and again,
oh my Love, my Only.
Searching for the other, searching for the Self,
  realizing that we were in each other all along, never separate.
How can the wave be separate from the sea,
a breath from life, and the fire from heart?
Our hearts are the organs of fire that ignite every night,
lighting the way for us.
Lighting the way for you dearest to find me,
  to find yourself, for me dearest to find you, to find myself.
Wake me up, oh my Beloved from this illusion of separation,
  and bring me into this magnificent love Divine,
  so I can stay there in the light with you.
So I can swim in the bliss of this love.
So I can be your Queen and you be my King.

CHAPTER FIVE

THE EGO DROPS TO THE GROUND

'...losing through you what seemed myself, I find selves unimaginably mine; beyond sorrow's own joys and hoping's very fears yours is the light by which my spirit is born: yours is the darkness of my soul's return: you are my sun, my moon, and all my stars'.

E. E. Cummings, poet and author

"And wherever you are is my home - my only home".

Charlotte Bronte

Ego story

At this point of your twin soul journey you are still telling yourself the ego story. Repeating it in your head, with all your fears and doubts about this connection. You feel this love in your heart and at the same time deny it in your ego. So the struggle continues, and from this struggle, the suffering occurs. The ego story you tell yourself is always limited because the ego cannot see the bigger picture. The ego is constructed in this way so that through suffering we get in touch with our hearts more quickly. While the ego identification is still present, you still believe its stories.

All the suffering comes from our false perception, which is not aligned with love.

We suffer because we project the ego onto another person or situation and we think that they must provide us with what we lack inside, but we do not lack anything, we are complete and enough always.

We see the world as we are, not as the world is.

The ego story you keep telling yourself about your twin and the connection goes something like this; 'maybe this love is not true? How could it be that a person who loves me so much doesn't even call or show their feelings for me? If we loved each other we would be together wouldn't we?' The story goes on and on, circling in your head, like all ego stories do.

In your inner dialogue you dissect and turn every word and sentence your twin ever said to you upside down trying to make sense of it all. You are going to toss and turn every word around like a worn out coin. You will not be able to match the beautiful feelings and words your twin spoke to you with the present situation. Your ego is going to put up a fight and not give up easily, but you have to know that the story it is telling you is not the truth. It is only a story trying to keep you from the truth. The more you start to understand and go deeper into this connection, the more the ego is going to torture you. This connection is a struggle between the ego mind and the heart's knowledge.

As soon as you absorb a new insight or knowing into your heart, along comes the ego to frighten you some more because your heart's truth is a death to the ego.

Its survival depends on your 'sleep' and unconsciousness and as soon as you become aware of the power of your heart's truth it becomes easier. Still, this journey is a struggle until you master yourself and become more conscious.

Suffering

As time goes by and you experience the physical separation, the running, and the chasing, you suffer. Suffer immensely. There is actually pain in your body around the heart chakra and solar plexus (your stomach) where you store all of your fearful emotions. The separation can sometimes take years, with the journey lasting ten, twenty, or even thirty or forty years in some cases depending on what you agreed upon with your twin and with some connections, there may be a complete cut of communication and physical encounters, while with others you may still be able to communicate with your twin occasionally. Every twin soul journey is as specific and unique as our souls are, and I think that there are not two same experiences but rather that there are points at which we all meet and those are universal.

Let me reiterate that this connection is not just a mind connection, as are most three dimensional relationships. It is not even between the mind and heart as are the more evolved relationships, but it is a mind, heart, and soul connection, the highest and deepest connection here on earth.

When you are in the separation phase, you cannot forget about your twin, you repeat every scenario between you that occurred on replay so often that at times it will feel you cannot think of anything else, and at this point, it gets a bit overwhelming.
You begin to believe that you are crazy and obsessed because you cannot understand logically what is going on and put things into perspective. You love your twin so much and feel the love of them so constantly that you cannot understand why it ended and why you should let it go.
This connection defies all logic because it has everything to do with your heart and the opening of it for another kind of reality that

nobody has taught you yet. You have to walk alone on this path into yourself, and although other people can give you pointers, it is ultimately up to you. This is the point when you suffer so much that you start to tell yourself the ego story about why the relationship cannot function, you start to lie to yourself that you do not love this person, you begin to invent a whole story based on your fearful beliefs. If you were in a higher conscious state at this point you could list all of your beliefs easily and clear them out in an instant; that is how powerful this suffering of the soul is. This suffering is like a spiritual thunder storm clearing you of all the negative charges in your body so that more light and peace can enter.

The soul will not let go, and knows and remembers the truth of who you are, but the ego will not give up without a fight either. Your ego wants to keep its reign, its rule, its false kingdom unshaken but this is not possible anymore. Because its foundation has begun to shake and at times so strenuously, that it collapses completely on the ground, asking what is going on.

Your ego can get confused as well, and if you are conscious enough you can predict every move it has. During this struggle you will experience temporary openings of the heart, for a few minutes your heart rules and your soul knows that that is the moment in which your beauty is at its finest, that you become this love. Your heart opens like the lotus flower but it closes again and this feels like a game of opening and closing.

Even if you have a glimpse of this heart truth and soul love beauty in this connection only for a moment it is enough, even if you are not yet fully awakened, it touches you in a way that you cannot be the same ever again.

These little glimpses or small awakenings are here for you to test the water, you open and then you close, you relax and you clench. It is an ongoing battle inside of you. You feel like the warrior in the midst of the battle, you do not know the territory and you have to find your way home, and this is no easy task.

The suffering on this planet is our state of being; it is our human condition which we chose for the contrast of experiencing how it feels to be 'out' of love, to be 'alienated' from love and to think that we have lost it. This is the experience of suffering, which can take many forms, but at the core of it all I believe there is a feeling of disconnection from love and our source, the God/Goddess force. It is the loss of remembrance about our origins and our descent, our core truth.

It is a deep sleep, from which we are for sure awakening at this time. In twin soul connection the suffering takes on another dimension of pain. Imagine the soul as a baby, pure and full of love and light, your most beloved in the world because it is who you are, and you reject this baby of light and love from your life because you feel deeply that you are not deserving of this bliss. I was meditating once when I acknowledged that I was refusing this love. I cried so much when this insight came to me and for the first time in my life I was truly compassionate to myself.

I saw clearly that we have to open the door when love knocks. I saw that it is not that we do not have love but that we do not let love wash over our being.

For the first time I saw this orphaned inner child and cried tears of love for her. That is the most excruciating soul pain ever, the rejection of oneself.

I would describe this pain as being as if somebody took all the beauty from you and put you in a cellar without light, and told you that you were never getting out of there. These feelings are not true in the higher echelons of perceiving.

Such is the game of ego at its most extreme, that it is only through the suffering that you can see what you are not, and can clear the way for your own liberation.

Temporary awakenings

Twin soul connection is a journey, a process of inner discovery, a walking home. This separation is a contract between you and your twin soul to experience the so called loss of yourselves, but later down the road you realize that you were never actually separated in the fifth dimensional state of being, and the illusion of ego begins to crack.

After some time the cracks start to be more apparent, until you break free from its shell. To me the ego construction looks like a shell we built around ourselves to protect us from something we imagined to be dangerous to our self-image. From what are we protecting ourselves? In reality we don't need the ego for protection, only for the practical and logical tasks in life. If we operate from our hearts there is nothing we need to be protected from, because all of those people who are 'negatively charged' towards us are already disarmed, or even better, they may not even be in proximity to us.

Ego lives in the duality of this world and we constructed it to experience both sides. Fundamentally ego is a shadow and the shadow couldn't protect us anyway, that is why when we acknowledge this we are free to observe it for what it is. Then you begin to lose your illusions.

You are the master of your life, of your true immortal, eternal, knowing true self, immersed in the God/Goddess heart and just playing a game of returning to this eternal self.

This whole earth experiment we call 'life' is a paradox and at the same time very intelligently played. For as long as we are in our physical bodies we shall never get rid of the ego and it is an outdated paradigm to think that because we assumed it is negative, we believed that we had to destroy it. In reality all you have to do is be conscious and observe and eventually embrace. When we embrace something we are not in the vibration of resistance anymore, so then we can vibrate with whatever we wish.

We transcend the ego with love and heart based consciousness.

We see it as the servant it is, it served a purpose to return us to love by showing us what does not feel good, and we thank it for that. Embrace the ego and shine upon it with love so it can never rule again. As soon as you see through this, it does not have a grip on you anymore. Then love starts to rule your life. There is nothing stronger than the energy of love in this Universe.
You lifted the veil and there are a few more veils on this journey travelling home.

Everything you have been taught to believe must be questioned while you go towards this emptiness of being where only love and pure potential is left.

All beliefs we carry within us are in a way only shielding the ego even if they are good beliefs. Because the ego can be so deceitful and can obscure a belief by wrapping it in pretty paper to make it look more attractive, but 'bad' or 'good', it is still a belief.

All beliefs are the death of intelligence, the kind of intelligence we all carry within. When we carry strong beliefs we stop ourselves from flowing; the flow of inner knowledge is ever changing, and a belief is always stagnation.

When you start to awaken you do not 'fall' so easily for the tricks of the ego any more, you see more clearly. In your physical life you start to talk less, you want to be alone to process all of these new feelings, you feel sad because nothing seems 'normal' any more.

This is completely ok. Feel whatever comes to you and be ok with it. Witness it.

At this stage it is hard to see the end of the road. Through my own experience lasting twenty-three years my twin and I have been mostly separated.

In these twenty three years I learned that this journey is predestined and that after your initial awakening you go back to sleep until you decide to wake up completely. The awakening happens in stages and cycles. Even when I decided to 'sleep' and run from this connection and be with other soul mates I never completely forgot about my twin. I just knew I had to go on and suppressed my feelings about our connection. In the year 2012 when many twin souls were meeting in the physical realm I met my twin after a period of almost ten years of no contact.

This 'chance' meeting was out of this world. It occurred in a hospital where both of us happened to be undergoing some check-ups, and when I stood there in front of him the feeling was so intense. I was in such wonder, awe, and left feeling speechless. I had an instant feeling of love, warmth, and safety. Time slowed down and we were in a bubble for those ten minutes. I experienced the same feelings as when we first met, the same intensity, although ten years had passed without contact between us.

Nothing had changed in our hearts because that is how strong twin soul connection is. The twin soul journey goes in cycles and as we know, it can go on for decades until both twins wake up.

Before this meeting happened, in 2009 he tried to search for me through a person we both know. He wanted to talk to me and to see me but I refused and told this person not to give my number as I did not want to see him. That was the ego speaking as I was feeling so hurt and angry at him. I wondered in my head what he wanted now after all these years and the thing which made it even more challenging was that I was in a relationship at that time and had kids. In my heart, I knew I wanted to see him. This time when he tried to contact me, in my heart I woke up a bit more and in my inner being I heard a whisper; 'this is true, this love is true'. The word REMEMBER reverberated through my whole being, but I still refused to consider this truth because I was not ready to face it myself.

I was still projecting on to my twin and blaming him for running, and not seeing that I was doing the same. At this point in my journey it was easier for me to reject him than to face myself; this connection is that powerful and crazy.

You attract each other like two magnets when you are aligned, and repel each other just the same when out of alignment. In your ego, as I stated previously, you think you invented this whole dynamic and that you are obsessive, possessive, or crazy.

It feels like you are wrongly locked in a prison and you are the only one who knows the truth of why are you there. You feel like you are the only one experiencing this. This feeling is very isolating, making you feel very alone.

Until the year 2012 I didn't even know about the concept of twin flames/souls. I was trying to make sense of what was happening to me, because after this meeting all the suppressed feelings came back and flooded me. The love was so intense that it took over my life. When I found out about twin souls, everything clicked and fell into place. I had the biggest 'aha' moment in my life. You know that feeling when you find an explanation for something that bothered you for a long time and you feel relief.

I felt like I had finally found the missing piece of the puzzle. You may even have a soul mate partner whom you love and who loves you but still there is a feeling that something is missing. This feeling is always there and it will not leave you in peace. It is a nagging feeling of emptiness, of long forgotten bliss, long lost love, a yearning for fulfilment and completion and it is the strongest call in this soul connection. It is a deep call from inside your soul to come home to your heart, to your twin. It whispers to you; 'come home, my beloved, come home'.

Your soul is a place where you belong when your heart opens and you hear your name called.

It is a journey

Whoever is on this twin soul journey will know this calling from a young age. The mission is felt even in your childhood and as a twin soul you feel different, you will feel that something about you is out of the ordinary. You will feel old, even at a young age.

You feel that you have experienced so much, and now you want to fulfil your mission and get out of here (Earth). You feel like you have experienced every possible soul mate relationship and you know that in this lifetime you will find that ultimate one, your twin soul. You know this deep within your soul.

I remember as a child that I always asked myself how come it was that I had a small body and yet I felt so old. I could not match my body with the feelings I had about myself. It feels strange when you are a child and you think there is one person out there made only for you. Often I felt like I communicated with someone and felt loved by someone whom I knew so intimately. I had an experience once when I think I was about ten, and we went on a school trip and there was a boy I liked and was drawn to him.

Later on through my journey I noticed that he had the same features as my twin, he was like a smaller version of him. All soul mate partners you encounter through your journey are going to have a fraction of your twin's energy. They will be somehow similar in physical appearance and in retrospect when you look at all your relationships you see that they were leading to your twin soul. You think all of these deep thoughts when you might be seven or eight, not consciously knowing much about love but subconsciously you know this truth, even as a child.

I was this *indigo child*, aware of the truth from an early age and one who never accepted the status quo in life. In my heart I could never accept that how people treated each other was all that there was in life and I knew that there must be a better way, a kinder and more loving way. A way of the soul love. A conscious way.

I had this knowing inside, this claircognizance and it was so strong and at times very hard to live with. Now, more and more super kids are incarnating at this time of accelerated ascension of the planet, to support and lead the change. These children show by example what love is and how we should relate in the future, from our hearts. They come with this knowledge and wisdom already inside of them.

These new children are highly intelligent, because they have lived many times on earth, and experienced so much. In this lifetime they just returned to be earth angels. They want to do this for their families and to return to this promised love. The majority of these kids did not incarnate here on earth ever, but came here from the more evolved planets and solar systems and carry this vibration frequency within them to enable earth ascension. When you are in the presence of these children you are being 'x-rayed' all the time. It is as if they bring the truth from within you when you interact. They allow no masks for you to hide behind. If you are on a twin soul journey these kids are helping you with your union and assisting you to raise your vibration. Many twin souls have kids with other soul mates and these children are helpers on their journey in many ways.

Unconditional is love from the heart of the God/Goddess to your heart, and I believe that the ultimate does not give promises that are forgotten, and unfulfilled.

Know this and surrender to this truth. I had a lucid dream once where just before awakening a Presence spoke to me in the most gentle and loving way and said; 'what is in your heart is a promise and you will see it fulfilled'. Sometimes you will meet your twin when you are very young, and sometimes you won't meet them until you are ready for full union because maybe in the 'previous' life you did all the work and now are ready. This is happening more often with younger generations, which I call the third wave of twin souls. I believe through my experience that twin souls incarnate in waves to help the ascension process, and at this time there are three waves of twin souls. Waves of twin souls mean that they incarnated on earth to cover a certain time span to help humanity.

The first wave are twins born in between 1940-1960 and now in their middle fifties to late seventies, the second wave are those twins born between 1970-1990 and are now in their thirties and forties, the third wave of twins are those born after 1990 and are now in their twenties. This is just the approximate division of waves and there can be exceptions before or after these years. Be aware that the first wavers and some of the second wavers didn't have the help of technology to obtain knowledge and more understanding about this journey, and for the third wavers it is much easier with all of the information available about twin souls.

However, all of the information can be also a trap if not used consciously. No matter what information you get from the outside, only you in your heart still know best about your journey. We are all together on this journey lighting the way for each other. At this time in society there have never been more divorces but at the same time, there have never been more people searching for true love. The high rate of divorce is happening because we are collectively evolving from the old paradigm of marriage and concluding the old karmic cycles.

The old paradigm of marriage was primarily of a financial nature, of security. The old paradigm of being married was also based on sexual attraction, matching the expectations of society, and above all, it was a karmic soul journey where we learnt most about ourselves and balanced our actions. We are evolving this old paradigm of relating now, and we want to connect it to sacred partnerships where the only motivation for us for being in a relationship is going to be love.

Twin souls with their tough journey are on the leading edge of the new, they are pioneers of the new sacred relationships. These new relationships will be reinvented in the future.

When you live with a soul mate and he or she is your mirror, showing you at what point in your journey you are, sometimes it is not easy and everything seems like hard work. We have worked so hard and now it is time to take it easier, to nourish ourselves, and to gift ourselves with the relationship of our heart rather than the conditioned relationships we were experiencing in the past.

The time has come for us to see that love should be the only motivation for us to experience a relationship and deep soul connection. No other motif should be of interest to you, not the looks, not the social status, not the education, not the ego personality manifestations, not the approval of other people, just love. Your only motif should be unconditional love.

Nothing should stand in the way of our hearts any more now when we are aware of this. I think we have had enough of compromising. It is time that we listen to our souls, and we will do because when we collectively awaken to this new reality and this new way of unconditional loving, we cannot go back even if we wanted to. We are awakening individually and collectively and twin souls are paving the way for everybody to see that real soul love exists, and that it is not a fairy tale as we are taught to believe. This love is true and alive, more vital and truer than ever.

Meditation
Changing your beliefs

The purpose of this meditation is for you to clearly see your beliefs and have the courage to change them. The other purpose is realizing your own power of creating your life experiences through the power of thought. Your thoughts have an electrical charge and send signals into the Universe.

Beliefs are nothing more than thoughts repeating themselves for a long time, which after a while become the dominant vibration in your experience. We all know that we humans are like walking receivers and givers of vibrations and as we go through our life we attract the matching vibrations. You can change these vibrations the same way as you created them.

Find a quiet, comfortable place where you can relax your body, sitting or lying down, whichever feels more comfortable to you. Find a place where you won't be disturbed for a while. Close your eyes and start to observe your breath going in and out of your nose. How beautiful it is to feel your breath of life and feel the life in you. Your breath is life flowing through you in every moment.

Now in your inner eye and inner vision imagine a white board. See yourself holding a magic pen and a magic eraser in your hand. Now start to write on that white board some of your beliefs about relationships, love, men, women, money, your body, or something you think strongly about. Whatever comes into your awareness write it down and do not censor it; whatever comes accept without judgement. Your subconscious is communicating with you now.

Now look at these sentences. They run your daily life, they are words or old programmes that you can change whenever you want. Take a deep breath and say; *'I am a powerful being and I can change and rewrite my beliefs at any time'*. Breathe in this knowing and peace.

Observe the energy in your body, how it feels and remember this powerful feeling of freedom to create. Now that you are conscious of these beliefs, you take a magic eraser and erase them all. Say to yourself; *'I am a powerful and creative being and I can create new beliefs for myself right now'*. Now take that pen and write with love, let love pour out of your magic pen for the creation of your desires. Write new sentences, which resonate with your new life from now on.

Be creative and loving and think about what a person who love themselves would write, how they would feel. Write about your perfect partner, about your best job, about your optimum body balance, about your highest potential in whatever makes you happy.

As you write, observe how you feel, how the energy feels in your body, and breathe, breathe deeply and with every breath accept this truth for yourself.

Now you know that you created something new for yourself. You look at that vision board and lock that image into your heart. Literally, you take the image and bring it into your heart. While you are doing this, you are giving your subconscious mind an order to operate from heart awareness, creating a new life for yourself. Be grateful for all of the abundance coming your way. When we create through visualization it is not enough only to visualize, but it is very important to open yourself to receive what is coming. Say to yourself; *'I ACCEPT all of the abundance in my life now. I ALLOW all of this abundance to come into my life now. I allow myself to RECEIVE. Thank you. Thank you. Thank you'*.

Invocation
Return to innocence

Oh, my divine love you journeyed with me through eternity.
We saw the stars give birth to the world together,
the same stars that sleep in our eyes.
When I gaze into your eyes I see them
shining brightly and fiercely.
Oh my love so sweet is the
remembering, do you remember this love?
How it made you feel?
It was real, yes, it was real.
That one second of recognition was all we needed,
to ignite our hearts on fire, and that fire burns and burns.
It will burn away everything that is not true,
For us my Beloved this fire is sacred.
We are sacred.
This love is the sacred heart of the Heart.

CHAPTER SIX

CRISIS AND THE TESTS OF ENDURANCE

'A soul mate is an ongoing connection with another individual that the soul picks up again in various times and places over lifetimes. We are attracted to another person at a soul level not because they are our unique complement, but because by being with them, we are provided with an impetus to become whole ourselves '.

Edgar Cayce, ' The sleeping prophet '

"The most beautiful thing we can experience is the mysterious. It is the source of all true art and science".

Albert Einstein

Pushing and pulling energy

Twin souls are drawn to each other like magnets, it seems one will always be running and the other chasing and vice versa, but this is just how it looks externally, inwardly they are both running.

As their individual growth continues simultaneously, they will have periods of balance and then they will attract each other immediately. At this point in your journey you begin to understand that because of the 'separation' you were thrown into yourself more rapidly. You understand that the separation was needed so that you could explore your inner world. Twin souls have the same soul frequency but have opposite polarities, so what actually occurs in the twin soul dynamic is the balancing of the polarities so that they can come together.

In the three dimensional reality this experience feels like a very deep longing for your twin soul even if your logical mind knows that the relationship is 'over' for the time being. There is a magnetic energy between the pair of twins and there is nothing

they can do to erase this feeling; this feeling of attraction exists even if they are consciously not aware of it. This pulling energy exists even if you try to shut it down.
This love lingers inside of you until you give yourself permission to embrace it and acknowledge it. In my own experience through this journey, the feelings became much lighter and easier when I truly admitted to myself that I loved this person with all that I have. In that moment I understood that all of these years I was fighting to keep this knowledge suppressed.

In this knowing, I understood how deeply we are conditioned to believe that we are not deserving of such magnificent love, of such unconditional love.

At the same time I acknowledged that to come into union with my twin, I must firstly believe deep inside of me that I deserve such a beautiful love and then consciously accept it so that this unconditional love can fully manifest in this three dimensional reality.

This twin soul love exists in the higher realms of existence and thus as you ascend and awaken to your true self you draw it all the way 'down' so you can both embody it. This is why it is so difficult because in this dense reality it takes time for something of such high vibration to get comfortable in the body.

You cannot understand why your twin is ignoring you and you feel like your energy is completely sapped for the benefit of your twin. It feels like your life energy is helping your twin to keep safe until you both come together in your hearts. You are each helping the other all along the way. Since you are one, this energy dance is always being felt and this does not make life easy.
All of these feelings of knowing are unconsciously perceived until the chaser wakes up one day and understands that they have had

enough, the pain is so great that it wakes the chaser out of this pattern of behaviour. Because they are at the end of their strength the chaser 'gives up' and goes on with his/her daily life. The chaser starts to understand that this game of chase does not work. In my own experience that was the time when I decided I had had enough, and that I wanted to engage with other soul mates, and get on with my life. Although what I was feeling in my heart was that this love is far from being over. At the same time what is happening with the other 'runner' twin is that they are awakening to this pain as well, and asking how could my twin go on with his life, when there is such deep love and connection? The fears of the runner twin are that their twin might abandon them completely and forget about them, or indeed they might fear that this love will never 'happen'. This dynamic continues between twins when the fears are not yet identified in both twins and so the 'runner' now feels deeply abandoned and betrayed by his 'chaser' twin.

The runner now thinks in their ego mind; 'if they loved me, they would wait for me'. When this inner realization happens in the runner, the runner might try to contact their twin just to make sure they are still there. They merely need the reassurance that the love is still here, they are just checking if the feelings of their twin are still the same.

They both experience a soul shock but in a different way, the chaser is shocked to realize that by 'chasing' he will never get his twin back, and the runner is shocked to realize that from now on he will have to go on without this dynamic of running.

This is shocking for the runner twin because it appears that their twin is giving up on them, but in reality, what is going on is that they are moving into their own self more deeply, so they can face their deepest fears. The runner twin knows subconsciously that he/she has to stop running and look deeper into his/her fears and is scared of it. This is like a game of cat and mouse, both running around in circles and both getting so tired that one day they sit down and stop in deeper awareness, exhausted and think to themselves; 'What is this? I cannot do this anymore, it hurts too much. Who am I chasing? Who am I running from? Who am I rejecting? What am I doing in my life? Who am I? What do I want?' All of these deep meaningful questions will be coming into your awareness and you will see more clearly into the pattern of this connection. You have never experienced something so deep, so soul searching, so painful and blissful at the same time. This connection is the biggest test of endurance that I know of from my life experience, because there is no 'proof' that you are not making it all up, but at the same time your heart keeps pushing you into your truth and in your heart you know you can't give up. This journey is a nerve wracking experience and it is also ego shattering, destroying everything you thought you knew about love. It leaves you spiritually 'naked' before your twin.

Remember that no matter how hard you try to hide from your twin you cannot achieve this because they know you on a deeper level, they are you, and you cannot run from yourself; in the end you are going to have to face yourself.

The crisis is so strong that it leaves you completely empty and you feel exhausted as if you have fought a long battle, you are satisfied that you did everything you could with the knowledge you had, but still dissatisfied because you feel you both 'lost'. But in this connection even if you lose you always win and it is a beautiful paradox. You constantly learn so much that it feels like the universe has sent you on a crash course of learning.

This connection teaches you the way of loneliness, the way of non-attachment, and most of all it teaches you how to love unconditionally.

You are this silent warrior, and you have a battle inside of you that is going to bring you home to your heart. I like to call all who choose this experience the 'navy seals' of spirituality because this connection is one of the toughest roads to spiritual awakening.

Your twin knows subconsciously that they love you deeply, but in this phase of the journey this knowing is not yet consciously recognized, because, as we saw, true love is scary for the ego.

The conscious mind tries to repress this knowledge so it does not have to deal with so many fears and limiting beliefs.

You have to be aware of the ego completely and acknowledge that it does not run the show any more, and that your soul is the master of this love and your life. As you slowly begin to accept this with clarity, the healing journey then begins. You start to see that your false self knows nothing about unconditional love and you start to surrender this love to the Divine.

The ego still operates but you are much more conscious of its game and the way it operates. It gets a bit easier now, but you still have to do the work and the journey still goes on. You must be prepared to confront your false self completely, be prepared to see your shadow clearly and acknowledge what is keeping you from your highest potential in life and the acceptance of this divine love. You must be brutally honest with yourself and this is not possible without the inner work. You must ask yourself constantly why you still hold a belief that you are undeserving.

This is the time when you dive more deeply into your unconscious behaviour. You are a witness now to your own psyche and you start to detach yourself from the ways of the ego and thank it for its efforts but you realize it is no longer needed and is now redundant. This is your own little personal victory and in your heart you know that you are ok. At this time, you are going to get additional help from all of the celestial helpers and the synchronicities are going to work in your favour even if you consciously still try to push this connection away. When you think you have no 'proof' in life that this connection is true, you are going to receive help.

Synchronicities are going to push you into your truth and ordained path more and more.

Synchronicities

Synchronicity is the concept first explained by psychiatrist Carl Jung, which holds that events are 'meaningful coincidences' if they occur with no causal relationship, yet seem to be meaningfully related.

Synchronicity is the way in which the Divine communicates with us in this three dimensional reality; in my opinion it is the most personal and most intimate language that God/Goddess has given us for expressing our joy in following our path.

Synchronicity is the channel through which the Universe is trying to deliver you a message. Grasp that, and you will know how important you are. Your growth is very important. The Divine does not let you give up on this love because it is what you came here to recognize and live by, and by giving you synchronicities the Universe makes sure you are always on track. In creating these synchronicities the Divine is very clever, creative and sometimes very funny.

The name of your beloved is going to pop up everywhere. You are going to hear songs that talk to you in a personal way, or which are meaningful for both of you. You are going to read books so evocative of your experience that it will seem that they speak directly to you. Messages are going to come from people who will say the most important thing you just then needed to hear, you will see shapes in nature that speak to you about union.

It will feel like the whole of existence is helping you to stay on your path. For example, in my personal experience I see the name of my twin everywhere, and it is not such a common name. I see shapes in nature that speak to me in sign language about our union.

Sometimes I used to ask myself how the Divine could manage to be so resourceful and creative, and I would be in awe. I used to hear songs that spoke to me and gave me the exact answer to the question I asked, or explained a feeling in me. I would see the shapes of eternity loops everywhere, numbers in combinations that communicated with me, books would cross my path that told me about love in such a way that was in accordance with my twin soul journey. Writings on billboards, walls, so precise that sometimes I was astonished. Movies too, because as a collective archetypal energy they are also a good medium through which you can obtain many answers.

Energy transfers can occur also, where you see somebody who reminds you of your twin and you feel their energy coming through that person. In these situations you will have a feeling that they are physically next to you. It is their way of comforting you while you are in the separation phase. These energy transfers happened to me a couple of times, and were one of the strongest, and most amazing synchronicities I experienced.

So many things are going to speak to you, and they are going to speak the most when you try to deny this connection, or when you are in doubt.

Synchronicities are going to be there to remind you. It will sound like God/Goddess is saying 'My dear one, you stepped off your path for a while and I am bringing you back, look at all of these reminders (synchronicities). My dear child just follow these signs and believe'.

To be able to experience synchronicities a person needs to be in a higher state of awareness, otherwise it will not be possible to decode the meaning, as these meaningful coincidences will not come to your conscious awareness enough for you to even register them.

To be able to see and experience synchronicities in your life you have to be awake.

Synchronicities are your personal symbols or omens talking to you from your own soul to ensure you are on the right path.

As you continue on your journey, they become more obvious, stronger, very creative, and persistent. When you wake up you will have a feeling that everything you experience in your life is one vast synchronicity. At one point, you will laugh and say; 'ok I get it, now you can stop for a while'. Synchronicities can get very reinforced, and sometimes it can feel as if you are being bombarded by messages, but those who are bombarded with synchronicities, I think, are those who are on the highest path. Synchronicities can be very humorous as well, and appear in unexpected places and in situations that seem to be serious, and then you realize that in creation nothing is serious but rather everything is loving and playful. Life plays with us if we decide to play with it; playfulness is a mutual game. So laugh with the abundant Universe where you are nourished, taken care of, loved, guided, and cherished like a precious child every moment of your life.

For your heart to make a beat each second, something is waking up in love every day and giving you this gift of life.

Be aware of your heartbeat and your breath, because this is the true gift of life. See this and follow your synchronicities. Follow your own path. It is your life and your personal unique experience of it.
Nobody else can experience from your perspective in the whole universe. There is but one of you, understand this truly and you

will never doubt your experience or worth ever. All of existence needed your unique perspective on life and that is why you are here. How can that be insignificant? So it is essential that you be authentic.

To be authentic is to see clearly your own experience of life and trust it, so that your love pours out to enable everybody to see their own authenticity.

When you are authentic, you are an expression of the Divine perspective and when you shine the light of your authenticity, you help others to see their own divinity in their lives too.

Dark night of the soul and the awakening process

The dark night of the soul (in Spanish; 'la noche oscura del alma') is a concept taken from a poem written by 16th century Spanish poet and mystic Saint John of the Cross.

He narrates the journey of the soul from its bodily home to its union with God/Goddess. This part of the journey is called the 'dark night of the soul' with the darkness representing the hardships and difficulties the soul endures during this period when it is detaching from the world and reaching the light, to go into union with the higher aspect of self and God/Goddess.

At this period in your journey, you might also be experiencing the dark night of your soul, where the unconscious within you is knocking on your door seeking recognition and acceptance.

Yes, the darkness can be accepted, and by embracing it, we can then transcend it. You are going to feel like you are dying and in a way you are.

You are spiritually dying only to be 'born again', releasing your false self and resurrecting into your soul. In my dark night my body collapsed totally and I was in bed for four whole days without being able to move, although I was completely healthy. I cried the whole time and it felt like I was standing on the edge of a cliff and no bridge was visible for me to cross over to where I felt my heart was calling me and turning back was not an option.

Those four days of being bedridden were just the peak of my dark night, but the 'dark night' lasted much longer. Dark night is just an expression for the state of the soul and it doesn't mean that the darkness lasts for one night only.

The period of your soul awakening into your light and true self can last for months or years, it all depends on how fast you let go of resistance towards your soul calling. It is a point in your life when you hit your darkest hours and it is hard. You might see no sense in anything anymore, you might experience sadness, lostness, and deep soul tiredness.

But know that dark night of the soul is not here to destroy you but only to set free your true self. Actually, it is there to destroy something; your false self, your ego structure, so that you can continue to live your life from an authentic place rather than from the conditioned state. It was the scariest feeling and the experience felt as if I had the spiritual flu, and a new me was trying to emerge. It was a powerful, profound spiritual experience. I learned from it that the dark and the darkest inside of us can be embraced, instead of being pushed further down into the unconscious.

We must bring the dark into the light of the consciousness so it can be integrated in order to unite the 'split' of good and bad inside of us. This is what it means to be whole (or holy).

Many of the great thinkers and mystics spoke about the dark night of the soul, one of whom is Carl Gustav Jung and also St John of the Cross whom I mentioned at the beginning. You can read and explore in more depth about this soul experience from these authors if you are interested. In this twin soul journey you are going to experience the 'dark night' at least once.

We all have been conditioned to be 'good' and deserving of love only if we behave in a certain way, but unconditional love teaches us that no matter what we do we are still deserving of love.

From the divine perspective this is how all of us are loved.
We are always worthy and enough. Because this twin soul connection is so divine, twin flames or twin souls feel like they are everything to each other. They are not just lovers but brothers, sisters, mothers, fathers, friends, children to each other and it feels that these expressions of love all come into one because this love is so sacred.
You are even closer to your twin than you are to your children, because your children are your closest soul mates, whom you love profoundly and unconditionally, but your twin is you, the same soul. You cannot be connected to any other soul more than to your own soul.
I came to the realization of this while I was doing a healing therapy session with one of my clients when she told me; '*I feel so guilty sometimes because my children cannot fulfil me, I feel like I love my twin even more*'. In my own experience, I felt this too, and this doesn't mean you do not love your children but rather you must know that this love does not have any limits. When I was feeling like this all of my guilt used to surface amidst all of the conditioning about how we should love. You love your children more than anything in the world and would do everything for them and now imagine a love that questions even that principle and shapes you to the notion that all should be loved like that.
The whole world should be loved unconditionally.

This connection trains you for the real manifestation of Christ's consciousness on earth.

It is *Divine love* manifesting as your soul on earth to show you that you are loved unconditionally, and that you can love others unconditionally too. There are no conditions you need to meet in God's love so that you can feel worthy of this love.

You are worthy just because you exist, if you exist you are already loved.

Sometimes in this part of the journey of opening your heart, you are going to close and open it on a regular basis because you are still afraid. Imagine a beautiful lotus flower representing your heart opening to receive the love and then closing for 'protection' again. When your heart chakra begins to open up you are going to cry often, this is especially true for men because they may have repressed tears for so long. You are still working on your fears and if you can see your heart as this beautiful flower you will see that when you are in that soul awareness mode your flower will remain open, and when you slip back into the ego, it is going to close. It is normal to feel this way, so you must just be gentle with yourself.

When you become aware of this pattern, it is going to feel completely different, because you will see exactly the times when or why you closed your heart down and it will not feel good anymore because now you are more aligned with your inner feelings and aware of yourself. You are watching yourself from a higher perspective and can see more clearly now.

That is the result of a beautiful journey of awakening.

You can picture the journey of awakening like you are climbing a mountain, and with every step upwards you see more of the valley and the view gets better and better, and you gradually see more and more. For most people awakening is a gradual process.

At the beginning it is most enjoyable because you are fresh and you have just begun your journey; you are full of enthusiasm and positivity. With the false viewpoint of your ego you think that you are better than people who 'don't work' on themselves, but be aware that this is just a trap of the ego. It is common at the beginning of awakening to think this because your ego has started to feel threatened by your research and experimentation and so by giving you feelings of superiority it keeps you in its game.

That is, until you climb some more and understand that everybody is 'working' on their spiritual path in their own way and that nobody is better or worse in their journey of awakening. By the middle of the climb, it gets harder and you get frustrated, as all of your shadows come knocking at your door.

It gets harder at this point, because your initial enthusiasm has passed and while you continue your journey, you do not know when it is going to end.

This climb takes all of your energy and your strength; it tests your endurance, your faith and the ability to trust, and so the middle part of the journey is hardest. When you start to approach the peak of the mountain you are already so 'crazy' that you start to doubt everything, and the talk inside your head goes something like this; 'why did I start this journey in the first place? I do not want this connection any more, I was better off enjoying my life without being conscious of this pain'. You start to question where this path is taking you, and if you are on the right path at all. You know now that this is your ego talking and the ego does not know the answers.

In this time of greatest doubt, it is the hardest to trust but this is the time you have to believe most in your path. Believe in just one more step, in one more insight, in one more synchronicity, in one more dream, and endure this feeling of not knowing, and trust in this journey.

Even the greatest of accomplishments and journeys were completed by taking one step at a time. All you can do is put one foot in front of the other and walk in surrender and trust.

The feeling of going crazy while awakening

The peak of the sacred mountain is very near and the 'valley of enlightenment' will soon enough be beneath you in all its magnificence and you are going to see the clear beauty of who you are. Yes, you are. We have this promise hidden in our hearts.
 I think whenever we are embodied and when God/Goddess says 'goodbye' to us for a while, then he/she sends helping angels to whisper a promise into our hearts to not forget who we are. Reminding us all along the way to know this love on an intimate level of our being, so that we can remember when we come to earth. We have been doing this for many lives and all of you who are on this twin soul journey have ascended before.
 All that we are doing on earth is awakening to this promise. We are REMEMBERING. Who and what are we remembering? Well, I think we are remembering our true selves and our beauty, our Divine origin.
 We are awakening from a dream of forgetfulness, but everything is ok because being the powerful creators that we are, we chose this experience. We are like these playful beings in the garden of creation where we choose in each second how we present ourselves. Even in the forgetfulness we are constantly creating, we are that powerful. This twin flame or twin soul experience is only one way among many paths of creative ways to seek for the divinity in our hearts. The first task of this connection is to bring you close to God/Goddess or the Divine intelligence. Souls can explore in so many ways that I think we cannot even imagine how many ways there are. Everything is a journey to the Divine heart, of which we are all a part. At this time, we are awakening to the game we chose to play and we are recognizing it more and more for what it is. This coming into our divinity seemed like a game we didn't like but now

we do not have to judge it anymore or ask ourselves if it is a good or a bad game; it is our creation and it is very intelligent.

A human being is no longer a slave to the Gods, but rather he is a fully embodied co-creator, creating together with the Divine. To be a co-creator means that we cannot do anything without divine guidance but conversely it means that the Divine also needs us in order to co-create.

We need to collectively awaken to this knowledge and only then will we start to experience peace. When we start to ascend and are on our journey to awakening, we start to vibrate with the truth of our inner being. Who or what is our inner being, you are going to ask? Well for me it is everything that resonates with the heart-based consciousness. We could say that our inner being is full of beauty, goodness, compassion, gentleness, the embrace of oneself and another.

For me that is truly who we are and what we crave for. The heart is so open when you awaken that every thought that you think that is out of alignment with the highest truth is going to hurt. You are going to feel this hurt in your body because you are becoming integrated and very conscious of the connection of the body, mind, and spirit. Sometimes I find I cannot grasp this feeling of so much beauty, the essence of who we all are. It is so pure, so innocent, so forever overflowing with love.

At the beginning of this awakening to love, as we have seen, we are going to feel very emotional and vulnerable, because we were shut down for so very long, and when these higher vibrations start entering our bodies, it can be painful. The body needs to adjust as well to these higher vibrations.

In our twin soul hearts as we awaken to divine unconditional love, we begin to see more and more the illusion in which we are living. We begin to see through the trap of society and organized religion where 'love' was forced into making contracts and was trapped by false promises. We, as the parents of our new earth children must ask ourselves if we are going to continue to encourage this lie by closing our eyes to true love. Or are we going to show the future generations by example what love is, how love should be expressed, and how love should be lived in the years to come. How should loving and unconditional relationships be reinvented for the future? We are building a new earth here and we have to bring down the walls that restricted us in the past.

We have to show our children, through leading by example, what love is. It is unconditional and free.

Meditation
Healing and balancing the chakras for divine union

The purpose of this meditation is clearing your energy centres for easier balancing and coming into union. Your chakras need to be rotating at optimum speed for the energy to distribute throughout your body.

In the ascension process, all chakras start to receive more energy in order to clear the blockages of old negative energy. When we feel pain, it is an indicator that the energy is blocked and wants to depart from a particular organ. Energy needs to flow through our bodies, and if chakras are blocked, the energy becomes stagnant. This meditation will assist you in clearing those blockages. On the path to ascension, we awaken all twelve chakras so that we understand the connection with the whole universe.

All awakened twin souls operate from a twelve-chakra system, unlike the usual seven.

Lie down or sit down, whichever feels comfortable for you. Find a calm space where you can be undisturbed for half an hour. Relax your body completely and start to breathe slowly through your nose. Start to observe your breath and breathe deeply a couple of times. Feel the sacred breath coming in through your nose and out through your mouth. Feel the breath of life streaming through your body, and know that you are alive right at this moment. Feel the now, the present moment.

In your inner eye and vision, see yourself sitting across from your twin flame and looking into their eyes. You are holding a shamanic drum and one of you starts drumming the beat of the sacred heart. With every beat of this drum, you are embracing and acknowledging this healing. Say silently to yourself or aloud; *'I call forth the one Omnipresence, God/Goddess and all the Ascended*

Masters, Spiritual guides and guides that help my twin soul union especially, to verify and protect this healing now. Let this healing be protected and guided in unconditional love and light. So be it'. You see yourself and your twin radiating and glowing from the inside, your whole body is flushed with this most beautiful golden white light, and it radiates out of your bodies. This healing is for your highest good, the highest good of your twin and all of the souls involved in this journey of union. Say this aloud or silently; 'Let all of the obstacles to this sacred union be gone now. Let all of the ego games of illusion dissolve in this unconditional love now. May we both see this connection as it is, pure and beautiful'. Amen.

This union is coming forth now in Divine timing and Divine perfection. Now lie down and hold your twin's hand, feel the energy moving through you in circles of the infinity sign. See all the chakras opening up like lotus flowers one by one, and clearing all the blockages of old energy. You can actually see these former blocking energies leaving your chakras one by one. Bring the beautiful white golden light through the crown chakra, through the third eye, throat, and into the heart. From the earth bring the beautiful red colour through the root chakra, through the sacral, the plexus, and into the heart and merge them together. As they melt in the heart space, they create a beautiful magenta colour of unconditional love.

 Feel this balance and peace. Ask your twin to put his hands on each chakra for the receiving and locking of this unconditional healing love. You repeat this process onto your twin as well. Feel the healing energy you hold together; you are powerful healers and when you are together that power is amplified. Now go further and see all the other five chakras opening; the one beneath you, your earth star chakra is glowing and connecting you to earth.

 Above you, your soul star chakra is connecting you and anchoring you into your soul, spirit chakra, universal, and stellar gateway chakra, connecting you to the whole Universe. You see all the chakras glowing in golden light. You feel light and empty of all that no longer serves you. As you go through each chakra, you see old energy and trauma clearing in the shape of smoke, blackened pieces of blocks, or liquid pouring from your sacral chakra into the root, and back into the earth where it is transformed right now.

You are healing in this very moment, and you should know that transformation needs no time but rather it is happening right now. Come back into this healing meditation whenever you feel like it to keep your chakras glowing in golden light, radiating health.

Stay in peace and breathe. Stay in your peace during the day.

Invocation
Feeling you

Through the dark you held me,
I was never alone, you were breathing through
my breath, you were beating through my heart.
You were holding my hand and my soul to keep it safe,
you told me everything is alright,
you told me that you are here watching over me.
Always feeling you in the wind caressing me,
feeling you as the rain washing over me.
Feeling you like a warm sun on my face,
feeling you in my dreams loving me.
Feeling you in my heart talking to me, oh, my Only.
There is never not feeling you, because I live through you.
You are more me than I am.
Through your love I am capable, I am beautiful.

CHAPTER SEVEN

THE DANCE BETWEEN TWINS

' He felt now that he was not simply close to her, but that he did not know where he ended and she began'.

Leo Tolstoy, Anna Karenina

*"So much, she loved the man,
so close and closer she felt herself that he became distorted in her vision like pressing her nose upon a mirror and gazing into her own eyes".*

Kendall Taylor (Zelda and Scott Fitzgerald biography)

Telepathic communication

*T*he word telepathy comes from the ancient Greek *'tele'* meaning distant and *'pathos'* meaning feeling, or passion. Telepathy is the experience of transmission from one person to another without using any of our known senses or physical interaction. Telepathy is an ability to communicate psychically no matter what the physical distance. While this twin soul journey continues, you are flying on the wings of love and Divine mercy more and more.

If metaphysical experiences like telepathy, visions, lucid dreams, astral travel (which can occur during sleep) and energy transfers are not occurring chances are that you are not in a twin flame union but rather in a more evolved soul mate relationship experience.

This whole twin soul journey is a mystical experience of high order and it awakens your intuitive and psychic powers.

As you go through this journey all of your dormant psychic abilities begin to awaken.
Some of these include:

> Clairvoyance (clear seeing)
> Clairsentience (clear feeling)
> Clairaudience (clear hearing)
> Claircognizance (clear knowing)

You might experience one ability as more dominant or you may find expression through the combination of a few.
Whichever way they manifest know that we are all born with psychic abilities and as we ascend and awaken, our 'other senses' become a normal part of our lives. As you spiritually evolve all of your senses are heightened and sharpened and you become very sensitive to the energies around you.
You will communicate with your guardian angels, and your spiritual guides, with this communication helping you on your journey. You observe your thoughts and feelings with clarity and only then do you start to see the agendas and beliefs of other people in everyday conversations.
You may have visions of yourself and your twin in meditation and your dreams become more alive, vivid, and lucid. Dreams start to speak directly to you. Your telepathy communication enhances, and you realize that you telepathically converse with your twin all of the time. Actually, this communication was there all the time, it is only now that you can clearly make a distinction between your thoughts and your twins' thoughts.

You start to develop this inner knowledge which at first feels very strange and isolating, because for so long we were dependent on religion, society, and now we have to stand alone in our truth.

When you are 'asleep' you behave according to the mass consciousness without questioning anything.

All of these current experiences are beautiful and mystical but at the same time they can be confusing until you gain a greater understanding of what is occurring. Telepathy between you and your twin goes on always whether you are aware of it or not.

From my experience I was not aware of this communication going on at the beginning, but then I realized that I was having conversations with him and that some of my thoughts were my twins' feelings and thoughts.

At the beginning, you will not know which thoughts are yours and which are not, but when you become aware you will easily see the difference between the two. You will sense the energy in your body, because when your twin speaks telepathically to you the energy feels somewhat different. When your twin wants to say something to you it will feel like their energy is coming into your inner space. You will feel their spirit being wrapped around you, either by your intense thoughts of them; feeling them beside you; or seeing their face in front of you. You will catch yourself having a telepathic conversation with your twin more frequently, and no, you are not inventing it. These conversations are as real as if you were sitting beside each other. At the beginning, you are not going to recognize this experience so often and you are going to doubt it, but as you go further into the connection it becomes so strong that it forces you to pay attention to it.

For all of these 'sixth sense' experiences you have to be awake and aware. Somebody who is unaware would never even register these experiences.

You can have a full, complete, beautiful conversation with your twin telepathically, and then you will start to see through the time continuum and the way we've been conditioned to believe in linear time and space distance. I used to find myself laughing when I realized that this conversation between us never stops. Once after we texted each other and the conversation had finished, all that was left unsaid in the physical discussion was spoken when we continued the conversation telepathically.

You will see that you can talk to your twin whenever you want. When you have a conversation with your twin in person you will feel like you are talking to yourself in the mirror.

Twin souls are just a micro representation of macro collective oneness, the representation of unity and wholeness. We are one ocean of consciousness, and inside that ocean, there is no distance and space between us.

The telepathy between twins is very strong; you can send thoughts and love to your twin and vice versa, and the love will be received and felt in the heart. During these talks, you are going to be in a relaxed dream state. This internal bliss will uplift your soul because you are helping each other through these conversations even if physically you are not together yet. In daily life, when you operate in beta brain waves you can still feel your twin, but when you relax and are in alpha and theta brain waves, telepathy comes in clearly. The communication between you never stops, you send and receive information to each other all of the time, even if you are not consciously acknowledging it as telepathy.

Know that a conversation or a contact in the earthly *Third Dimension or 3D* comes after all this has already occurred in the astral *Fifth Dimension or 5D*. I know how strong the illusion of separation can seem in the three dimensional reality, which makes you believe that nothing is going on, but there is always something going on even if you cannot see it in this reality. This is how you know so much about your twin and it is no surprise that when you meet in the 3D that you already instinctively know things about each other. This connection is unbreakable and as you go through the day, you talk to your twin.

Telepathy is an ongoing dialogue between you, regardless of whether you try to shut it down or not. You might be busily going about your day, but at the back of your mind the conversation is always on, and when you relax you 'pick up the phone' again.

That is why at night time before sleep you feel your twin connection intensely because all of your 'guards' have shut off during this time of relaxation and so it seems that then you are thinking of your twin even more. You help each other all the time. Your twin has your back at all times, and that is beautiful to know.

Dream world and 'past lives'

A dream is a state of withdrawn waking consciousness and of entering another dimension of consciousness.

Dreams are the space into which we enter, where we perceive images, feelings, and sensations, when we are not in an ordinary waking state of consciousness. When we are approaching sleep we enter into slower and slower brain waves until we drop into delta waves. When we sleep we are not affected by our ego-self and we can go deeper into ourselves without the ego trying to censor our experience. Dreams are the realm where you meet and communicate with your twin. You are often going to dream of your twin where you send messages to each other through dreams. You can travel multi-dimensionally and visit the places of your previous incarnations.

As you experience these dreams, you can consciously heal in a lucid dream with your twin.

Only your healed heart can touch the heart of your twin to heal his own, and to find the love inside.

Open up to dreams as they can teach you, heal you and show you parts of yourself that you need to understand. Your twin will come to you often in dreams and give you messages about your union. 'Past lives' are your experiences from multi-dimensional realities, meaning that if there is no linear time, all of these realities are occurring at the same time. You have loved each other through many life times, and many of the 'past lives' will be revealed to you through dreams. If you are spiritually awake you can spontaneously experience past lives through astral travelling in a dream state, in deep meditation, or you can have a past life regression therapy.

I put the term past lives in quotation marks because if we think in non-linear time, past lives are not past but are occurring all at the same time, in the eternal now. In the soul, all of our experiences, whether being past or present are 'recorded' and by tapping into those experiences we can make sense of our patterns, habits, likes and dislikes, or our fears. We, as humans, are so much more than we sometimes think and we have an infinite amount of recourses inside of us for understanding ourselves and making our lives abundant. <u>I like to call past, present, and possible future lives, parallel experiences as well.</u>

Imagine many timelines where all of these lives, past, present, and future, already exist and you are tapping into all this soul wisdom and knowledge. Through past lives you are going to heal tremendously and gain understanding about your soul and your life journey. You will learn about your talents, lessons you have to learn in this life, and about your soul purpose.

You have shared several lives with your twin soul and this is why it is very important to be conscious about your past life experience. Through past lives you will learn so much about your union, who you are to each other, and why some things happened the way they did. You will learn to see a bigger picture in your twin soul journey and connect the dots in your present life. In other words, you will have a greater understanding about your twin soul union and a profound healing can happen which will help you to come into union. To believe in past lives is not an imperative here. What is more important is your willingness to be brave and curious enough to explore your consciousness, for when you experience something like this for yourself, great insights and knowing can come to you to transform your life.

I had a few past lives together with my twin which I am not going to talk about in detail here because it would take too long and maybe it would make a good subject matter for another book, but I just want to say that those experiences gave me so much healing and understanding about myself, my twin, and our union. The therapeutic value of experiencing past lives and releasing all blocked emotions is tremendous.

When you experience 'past lives' you will learn and heal so much through these revelations. Through these experiences you will understand that love is not merely a concept; love is truly alive and real.

If we ask all the time if there is a God, we do not intimately know love. By God I mean the God/Goddess qualities which are present in all of us, since we are not in any way separate from the God/Goddess. Love is God, and God is love. There is no other God than love.

A vulnerable and gentle heart is a place where God lives. When we truly love we feel open and vulnerable. You don't need concepts or beliefs to find God/Goddess; you have your soul, just enter its kingdom.

In my personal experience the most significant heart awakening for me was when my twin visited me in a dream, which happened a week before we would meet in the physical sense in 2012, at a time when many twin souls met. We were in this 'past life' and there was a scene where he came to me and he put his hand literally on my heart and said to me; 'this is mine, it was mine and is forever mine'.

At that moment, I awakened in a dream and I just knew that I was not dreaming but I was experiencing another multidimensional reality. It was so lucid that it felt more real than the bed I was sleeping in. It was so vivid and colourful and I was so conscious in that dream that it felt as if I was in a movie scene and knew every word and movement. I knew at that moment that he was calling out for me to awaken.

My heart was accepting so much light in that instant, I felt as if the love could burst forth from my chest and embrace the whole world, so beautiful and mysterious was it. When I woke up from the 'dream' I needed some time to distinguish between the various realities and I knew that something profound had happened. He literally woke me up in a dream and dreams were never the same for me again. I awoke to this new reality and I now believe we see these realities all of the time but we are not conscious of them. You know that feeling before you wake up and for a few seconds you do not know where you are, and you have a feeling that dreams and waking life blend.

We are so conditioned to believe that a dream is a dream, and separate from this 3D reality but in truth it is not. It is just an extension of life or another side of the mirror.

A dream is just a screen behind the mirror. I perceive the dream world as a very thin veil, and if you are conscious and you wish to, you can choose to look through it any time you want. When we dream, our conscious mind shuts down all of the beliefs and programs so we that can perceive another kind of reality.

We can be more awakened in a dream, than in this 'dream' we call reality.

Don't forget that we spend a third of our lives sleeping, that is on average 33% of our lives or 26 years, and it stands to reason that dreams have a big purpose in our lives. There is no difference between these realities, the only difference is the state of consciousness from where you choose to observe them. Who made us believe what is real and not real anyway? In the awakening journey, the so-called dreams can be more real than the dream reality in which we live and call life. The dreams can teach you about who you are; they can show you your talents, heal you, and help you in so many other things.

To awaken means to find your own reality and your own truth and live by it.

Once when I was in so much pain that a genuine prayer came out of me, and I cried; 'if this love is true, show me tonight'. That same night he came to me in a dream and told me; 'this love is so real, this love is so real'. He kept repeating it until we both cried with so much love while holding each other. I felt that night that nothing would be the same ever again. All of my channels opened more and more from then on and I started to trust this journey completely.
You don't need authorities to give you approval so that you can trust yourself. You are the authority you have been waiting for, and there is so much freedom in this statement. Since twin soul experience is perceived and felt in the fifth dimensional reality, and operated and lived from an even higher dimensional reality at times you are going to feel doubtful.

As there is no 'proof' in the third dimensional reality for what you are experiencing you are going to feel alone and 'crazy' sometimes. Be aware that this is just your old ego crumbling away, and I think you already know that you are not crazy. You are not crazy.

Occasional meetings in the 3D

The perfect orchestrations or the divine interventions are always at play in twin soul connections and on those occasions, you can meet your twin by 'coincidence'. You know of course that there are no actual coincidences in this universe but instead there is synchronicity and connectedness of all. These meetings wake you up even more.

These meetings are always good for both of you and every time you see your twin, your love is grounded in this dimension even more. In my personal experience, while I lived abroad for a number of years, every time I would come home for a visit, maybe once every two years, each time without fail I would bump into my twin on the street when least expecting it. The city I live in is not a village let me tell you, it is a city with a population of one million.

Therefore, it begs the question, what are the chances of these meetings happening? It was like this every time without exception, until I started to awaken to the truth. Every time you and your twin are in close proximity, even if it is just crossing the street close to each other, something happens deep inside of you on a molecular level. You are going to be put 'close' to each other many times even if you don't meet face to face. You are always 'near' each other.

In one particular meeting with my twin I saw him crossing the street from a distance, and my whole body started to shake and I felt this beautiful warmth around my heart and stomach. It was so strong that I had to take notice of this feeling; I could not ignore it. At the time in my ego's mind I thought that this feeling was probably the sort of butterflies you have in your stomach when you see someone you loved from before, but little did I know then, that it was the raising of the kundalini in that moment.

I remember as if it was today when I asked myself; 'Oh my God, how can my body react so strongly to someone that I haven't seen for so long?'

Without knowing it, both of you orchestrated these meetings on a higher level and each time you meet the cells in your body start to trigger the remembrance of your contract and mission.

> When these meetings happen, time always slows down so that you can perceive more deeply what is going on; it feels as if the outer world shuts off and you enter into your body so you can feel the sensations.

Imagine that you are watching a movie and all of sudden it begins to transmit in slow motion and so it was another time when I saw my twin pass by and I felt like I was in a slow motion movie for a few seconds. When you are finished you 'come back' again. On these occasional meetings, your cells are literally awakening and starting to remember the love between you and your twin on a deeper level.

Nothing is what it seems on the outside, and in the ordinary every day, mystical initiations take place without you even knowing. It is all beautiful and guided by the Divine.

Rising of kundalini

Kundalini meaning 'coiled one' in yogic philosophy, is the primal energy located at the base of the spine, and you can preserve this life energy for accomplishing your mission. Kundalini or life energy is the life creating force that can be used for much more than sexual expression. Usually it is in the dormant state until you start to spiritually awaken. The best explanation I can give from my understanding of this dormant force is that it is the creative potential of us humans. It is the intelligence of complete spiritual maturation. Kundalini is the touch of the Holy Spirit, Sacred Fire, Christ Energy and it doesn't matter what name we call this energy, what matters is it's purpose. When you are on your ascension path the kundalini life force energy can be felt literally, going through the body upwards and downwards. The Sanskrit word *kundalini* means coiled like a snake. Because this word is overused by so many people it is considered almost a myth or a legend. Yet those of us who know from experience what the rising of kundalini energy is cannot possibly consider it to be a metaphor. It is quite literal.

What the rising of kundalini can do for your life is of enormous benefit. It can change you quickly and there is no need to put a mystical cloak around it, because it is the God/Goddess life force with which all of us humans are born. Everyone has access to it if they so wish on their spiritual path.

The important thing to realise is that you do not have to force your kundalini to rise because it will happen naturally as you progress on your spiritual path.

Kundalini energy can make your spiritual path smoother, your personal mountain easier to climb and can act like a sword for that extra push to enable you to cut through your years of conditioning.
It is a sleeping creative life force at the base of your spine waiting for your invitation to arise. As you progress through your journey and become more awake, you can actually feel this energy moving through your spine and body, and you can transfer it to whatever body part needs it if you so wish. That is how powerful a creator we are, with this elixir of life, this power inside of us. When you meet your twin in the physical, every time the kundalini energy climbs

up through your body, you can literally feel it moving through your spine. The feeling is somewhat similar to sexual excitement but it is not identical, as it is combined with goose bumps on your skin, with the Sacred fire warming up your body from the inside, while you get chills down your spine.

It can be nauseating and dizzying if you still need to purge and heal, and symptoms can vary from person to person. It is quite hard to describe it as it is with all spiritual experiences, because mere words do not do justice to the actual experience. I like this expression and it is so true for me; 'when it is spoken it's already gone', and so it is sometimes when we try to explain our spiritual experiences. We keep our deepest soul experiences in our hearts and we know our truth.

> *As we become more and more aware and awakened we don't require 'proof' that something is true for us. We know our own truth and we own it. That is the true spiritual revolution and in this revolution we trust our hearts so much that we become our ultimate authorities. That is true authenticity.*

Do not confuse authority from an ego point of view with true spiritual authority. The difference is that the ego authority is only interested in power over others, but an awakened individual who knows that he is his own authority, is interested in respecting all life, and is interested in cooperating with others for the benefit of all. Your twin soul, your ultimate mirror, is helping you among other tasks to raise your kundalini, because when you work in unison, you work on all of your energy bodies, which must all be in harmony. Even when you are not conscious that your twin may be nearby, perhaps only two streets away, the energy is still strong as I can recount from my own experience.

On another occasion as I was walking down the street I felt the same sensations of kundalini rise and thought to myself; 'how strange this is', and after five minutes passed I saw my twin again by 'coincidence'. Incredibly, my body reacted five minutes before I saw him. This is a beautiful dance between twins and indeed what a blessing it is to come back to your heart based-consciousness where you understand this truth.

You will have lots of 'aha' moments of recognition and a growing knowledge that whatever you try to do guided by your ego, or whatever you try to create from your limited awareness, does not work in this connection. You will realize that there has never been a separation, and that your beloved was with you always. As the wonderful Rumi, one of my favourite poets said; *"The lovers do not finally meet somewhere, they are in each other all along"*. What a profound truth this is.

Meditation
Feeling the connection and the unconditional love

The purpose of this meditation is to show you the power of this love; its purpose is also for healing your heart together with your twin and releasing the blockages that keep you from union.

All of the things that keep you from coming into union must be cleared beforehand, so you can enter like royalty into the temple of love. This meditation can help you stand in your own sovereignty knowing that this love is within you.

Find a calm and peaceful place where you will not be disturbed for half an hour. Sit or lie down, whatever feels more comfortable. Begin by closing your eyes, and relax your body and mind completely. Breathe deeply a couple of times, inhaling through your nose, and exhaling through your mouth. With every breath you take, your body is more relaxed. Be aware of your body and feel it touching the surface, feel the contours of your body filling the space of the room.

Now in your inner vision see a beautiful waterfall. Listen to the sound of the water; it is a beautiful spring day. The nature surrounding the waterfall is magnificent, all green, and lush in vegetation. You feel the scent of flowers all around you, you are there in complete peace breathing in the sweetness of this scene. Your body feels lighter than air and you are aware of everything around you. In front of you your beloved twin soul is standing. You smile at your twin and they give you the most magnificent smile in return. This smile feels like the sun is shining on you. You are at peace and feeling calm and full of love.

You feel these magnificent surroundings around you, the beauty of nature; you sense the cleansing power of the water in front of you. You are standing facing each other, and now feeling this energy and love between you. From your heart, you see that there is a beautiful golden thread going into your twin's heart.

You see it is glowing and pulsating with energy, and as it circulates it closes the circuit of love in an eternity shaped loop. Feel the love opening your heart and pouring this unconditional love into your entwined hearts. This energy feels like electrical impulses through your bodies. As you send love, at the same time you receive love and you experience this sacred eternal flow of Divine Love. You say silently or aloud; *'I receive this love now from my twin, and at the same time, I give this unconditional love to my twin. I am worthy of this unconditional love.*

My heart is open to receive this love completely. So be it'.

The infinity sign is a sign of no end and no beginning, it is eternal like your love. This is endless love. Feel this and if any emotions come up, feel them and release them, and stay centred. You can write down what you experienced. Bathe your being in this love and breathe. When you have experienced enough be thankful in your heart for this Divine connection.

Know that this love is always with you, there is no separation. Stay in peace and truth during the day. Connect to this love during the day or whenever you are in doubt or having a hard time, or whenever you want to feel close to your twin. You are always connected in this love.

Invocation
Love is all

You love me as the sun loves the moon,
every night the sun hides, so the moon can shine.
I know this love. I feel this love.
You kiss me as the sea kisses the shore,
it pulls and pushes against the shore kissing it constantly.
I know this kiss, I feel this kiss.
How you love me my love, so tender is your love.
You cherish me like the porcelain bird,
on the palm of your hand.
You breathe me like the air, and cleanse me like the wind.
Blowing through my bones, you take everything
that is not love.
Then only love remains, only love is.
I know this love, I feel this love.
Love is all, when you love me.
Love is all, when I love you.
You came into my dreams to awaken me from a dream,
You touched my heart so I would not forget who I am.
I bless this love, I bless you, I bless myself.
May we be blessed, in this love, oh my Beloved.

CHAPTER EIGHT

COMPLETE SURRENDER OF EGO
-Surrender stage-

' Oh Vittorio, I have tried so hard to get her out of my heart '.

Father Ralph, Thorn Birds

*"Come away, O human child:
To the waters and the wild
with a fairy, hand in hand
for the world's more full of weeping
than you can understand".*

WB Yeats

Seeing through the ego game

This beautiful, and at the same time challenging path of twin souls that you chose is dividing you from inside out. It is breaking the ego shell that you have built through millennia. This shell was formed from layers of false beliefs about the world and about life. All of these false beliefs created this shell for the purpose of survival, of 'protection', from this world. Now it is time to break out of this shell and set yourself free.

As true spiritual warriors, we know that we do not have to fight for survival when everything is given in love, we do not have to compete because we are all one, and we do not have to protect ourselves because we are held in the palm of God's hand, and are protected always.

When we start to see through this ego game that we have been playing for so long, some of us will have had enough and we will want to experience something different. Let us say we want to play another game, and let us say this game is one of spirituality; it is all new, and exciting. Do not be caught up in a game because in this awakening process ego can be very intelligent and deceive you into thinking that you are 'more spiritual' than other people but that is not our spiritual truth because we are One Source Love. When you believe anything for a while you are stuck, even if that belief is not harmful.

The best thing you can do for yourself on a spiritual path is to not get stuck for too long in any belief, if possible.

Observe yourself constantly and keep your beliefs in check. Just keep flowing. In addition, know that it is all a 'game' even if it is a spiritual game you want to play. The one who chooses to stay unconscious serves the whole just the same. There is no judgement whatsoever on a path somebody is choosing from their own unique perspective.

The only thing we have to focus on as individuals is loving our own hearts so much that we radiate our love and happiness onto others.

In this way we can affect those around us by emanating peace and compassion from our own hearts. I think this truth is the core of what Gandhi meant when he said; *'You must be the change you wish to see in the world'.* If you want to change the world, first change yourself. See yourself clearly. Change your thoughts, change your heart, and change your perception of the world that surrounds you.
We cannot any longer preach about what we are not becoming ourselves. That old paradigm of functioning is going away, and

now we are called each day to contribute as individuals. The ego's mind will tell you that as an individual, you are powerless to change anything, but you know that this is false because if each of us did something we would change this earth very quickly. In the midst of twin flame soul challenges, can you see clearly what is stopping you from opening your heart wide and having this unconditional love? You guessed, it is the ego.

The ego is telling you a story in your head, only to keep you from listening to your heart, but as a more conscious being, you are observing its mind games and making heart-based choices more and more. As a conscious human being, you have two choices when you approach any decision in your life and these choices are your head versus your heart.

In each situation when you are in a dilemma you have to ask your heart what it would desire to do in that situation?

What would a person who loves themselves choose? You know what the other choice is. To tell the difference between your ego and your heart you have to be aware so that you can observe your feelings.

Your feelings are indicators of whether you are choosing from your heart or your ego.

The ego makes you feel powerless, deceitful, doubtful, guilty, hating, and ashamed. Your higher angelic self and your soul provide you with the complete opposite. When you make a decision out of a space of love, you will feel love, security, peace, calmness, empowerment, self-confidence, and lightness.

A conscious person knows how they want to feel and they consciously choose the thoughts that make them more aligned with their heart.

Yes, you finally see that you can choose from this menu of different thoughts and create feelings, and thus you can start to live any reality you want.

Sweet surrender and shadow side

What most people perceive as surrender means being weak, powerless, and deciding to be defeated. This could not be further from the truth. The true meaning of surrender is when you are so completely in your heart and you willingly decide to 'give up' on your dreams and desires so that the Divine can play its part in assisting you to recreate them.

Surrender is your full cooperation and co-creation with the Divine force to create miracles in your life and the lives of others. In other words, you surrender to your higher self and you no longer want to play the game of ego, because you know that a limited perception can never bring unlimited results. Surrender is giving up control on the outcomes in your life and your twin soul journey. As you surrender you slowly start to feel the complete beauty of this celestial love and protection. This soul Union is protected and by surrendering it to the Divine infinite intelligence you are moving yourself 'out of the way' so true miracles can occur. As you journey through this twin soul experience you will 'be asked' to surrender many times, until you finally 'give up' on your ways of making it happen. Slowly you start to integrate and love yourself on all levels, because you realize that the pain needs to be addressed not pushed away.

Your twin pushes you to address everything that you wanted to leave 'hidden under the carpet'. Nothing can be left hidden in the dark or kept secret from your twin.

The light of your united hearts shines on every corner of unaccepted parts of yourself and tells you that you need to love every part until you are fully integrated and balanced within. This experience is so difficult because for integration to take place we have to dig deep into our shadows and love them for what they are. For too many of us, this can seem frightening but it is scary only from the perspective of the ego ;when you actually begin to do this you see that light is always embracing and accepting of all parts of you. When you go through integration, do not be disheartened because even when you are in the middle of the darkest of nights the light is always there.

When you embrace your shadow, there is no more division inside of you, between the good and bad. You start to become whole.

You become aware that everything is not just black and white but that there are so many beautiful colours you did not see before. You start to see through all of the judgments you put on yourself and others and how deep those judgements go. At the same time you start to judge yourself less, and as you do that you see that, likewise, you judge other people less also.

When we judge the other we always judge ourselves, and we take away a part of love we could have given to ourselves by projecting something negative onto another. Instead of embracing and loving a shadow aspect of yourself, you project it onto another person, by not liking something in them or about them.

By judging, all we do is escape from ourselves; it takes a conscious person to see clearly that whatever you judge in someone else, there is an aspect of that in you, even if it is never manifested in physical form, existing only in our thoughts or energy.

*I believe the highest expression of love is
non-judgement and compassion.*

Think of the deep conditioning we have been through, of rejecting our shadow side when obviously it exists. The shadow side doesn't have the same power over us when we unleash the love into it. We cannot reject the shadow any more but embrace it with love. It is a true heart's way, the one way we humans must take in order to make that jump from ego to heart and cross that bridge from animal to God/Goddess. We are these ever-evolving and changing beings on a journey back to source. The heart way of being is choosing each moment from your heart, and making decisions in your life from that space.

Healing is about making the unconscious visible to yourself and loving it, loving whatever arises from it in the moment, instead of suppressing and rejecting it.

Most people think of healing as a one-off episode of hard work that you undertake and then you are done. This is not true, from my experience, because as I was asking myself; 'when I am ever going to heal?' I found that there were always new layers to heal and accept. I like to think of healing as a process whereby we see all of our 'faults' clearly and still know that we are whole. To heal does not mean to be perfect but rather 'whole', meaning that you accept all of yourself, both shadow and light.
For example, you could be very nervous and yell at somebody who didn't deserve it and feel guilty afterwards but instead of marinating in that guilt you can touch your heart and love your guilty self, and go and say sorry to that person that you have offended. You can breathe and be conscious in that moment, and create a different scenario every next moment. When we are conscious, we always have a choice about how we wish to act in a certain situation. You are not a 'loser' if you choose to walk away

from a violent scene, if you choose not to return the insult to the person who treated you poorly, but rather you are conscious that their behaviour is not yours, that their behaviour has to do with something unconscious in them. If some situation is challenging for you, you can touch your heart and love it, and when you cannot go on any more and you feel you don't know how, love some more. Strip and strip away some more layers of your false conditions. Set your own rules, set your own course to the stars. When we start to love our shadow self instead of resisting it, it becomes obvious that it is really a shadow. There it is, scary and big but not real. We have to be aware that we can choose every time.

Through the recognition of conscious choice, we are liberated.

We see that we have always been free. Free to choose.

Believing yourself

The power is yours, know that. We are conditioned in this society to think that the unconscious is frightening and very hard to bring to light, and if you touch that dark part of you, you could cross the sanity line. What does it mean to cross the sanity border? Where is the border between being crazy and sane? We all know that the line is very thin, and that all of us live in our own worlds and we could say we are all crazy in a way. What is normal? The normal is considered to be the standard by the consensus of the many, but we all know that what the majority agree upon to be normal is not always so.

When an unconscious human being tries to grasp the shadow, he has divided feelings of trying to understand and to reject it at the same time. He suppresses so much information into his unconscious, and when the split happens between the conscious and the unconscious the 'border' is gone. This is where insane people live, in between the two worlds. When a conscious person tries to grasp the shadow he is a mere observer, he does not identify with it, he just acknowledges it and embraces it.

He throws all the 'garbage' into the bin where it belongs. Thanks to all the brave explorers of the soul who lived before us and who gave their lives for their heart beliefs we know better today. We know that we don't need external validations for our experiences. We trust, we know, and we go. Today we live in a beautiful time of change although it is sometimes hard to see on the outside where the change is becoming visible. This change is happening on the inner plane first and ripening in all of us, until it is ready to manifest in the visible.

As we individually wish for something to manifest, we wish it at the same time collectively and when a large number of people wish the same, our reality starts to change.

We have to put a collective wish out there for it to manifest. So the question remains; 'What is your individual wish for the raising of the vibration of love on this planet?'

The heart way

The heart way is waiting for all of us in this new dawn of awakening to our divine selves. The heart way is calling many of us, and this means that we are going to be fully aware and conscious about our choices, and we will choose from our souls more and more. We will be fully aware and free to choose how we want to live our life. The heart has its own intelligence, as does the mind. The heart is the electromagnetic field generator that thinks.

The electromagnetic field of the heart is 100,000 times stronger electrically and 5,000 times stronger magnetically than the brain. We are so used to thinking only with our mind but we should use the intelligence of the heart as much as the mind, if not even more. We are not bodies having a soul experience but rather souls having the experience in the body. If we follow our heart wherever it leads us, our heart can take us to the highest potential of our souls. We are not going to sell our integrity any more for false security, money, prestige, appearances, or social status, but rather live and do what we came here to do, first individually, and then collectively.

Our heartbeat is synchronised with the heartbeat of the Universe; we only have to turn the ego volume off, so that we do not hear the noise of the mind so much and hear the heart more clearly. The rest will be easy because the current of our hearts will guide us.

Meditation - Exercise
Writing a letter to your ego

This meditation exercise is about seeing your shadow self clearly, it is about accepting the parts of you that you do not like. This exercise will help you to integrate more easily the parts of the unconscious that are suppressed in you. You can do this exercise daily and its powerful effect will be visible in your life.

Find a peaceful and calm space. Sit down comfortably because in this exercise you are going to write. Light a candle or incense, and create a sacred space for this ritual. You can listen to some beautiful, relaxing music if you wish so. Breathe deeply a couple of times so you can enter a more relaxed state. Relax completely and be thankful to spend some intimate time with yourself.
 For this exercise, you will need a paper, a pen and a candle. As you breathe deeply say to yourself; *'I invite everything that I do not like about me and in me to the light of the consciousness now'.*
Light a candle and start writing a letter to your ego as if it is a person who you cannot stand very much. Write all that you judge, what you don't like about yourself and other people in your life. Put that inner dialogue out onto the paper. Start writing and be honest, and whatever comes let it go. Do not censor anything you have to express. Write whatever comes and trust the process. At first when you start writing you will be scared and surprised at all that was suppressed in you, but as you go along you will feel lighter and lighter. You must acknowledge and observe all that the ego was trying to do, observe where the shadow is running your life, be aware.
This exercise is not for judging the ego but rather being conscious of the traps of the ego that we fall into. Whatever you write, accept. The list can be long or short, whatever comes in this moment, accept. Just breathe and know that you are always safe and ok, no

matter what. When you feel that you have experienced enough, say thank you to your ego which has served you so well, and helped you to know who you truly are, because through who you are not, you find out of more of who you are. Such is the game of duality we choose. We learn through contrast.

Be thankful because you are the creator of your experiences. When you are finished, you take this letter and burn it so that the sacred fire can transform the shadow into the light. This way you are giving an order to the subconscious mind not to fear the shadow.

Stay in this awareness, breathe deeply, and say aloud; *'I see my false self clearly and embrace it in my higher self-understanding and healing now. I am, I am, I am the truth, the way and the love'.*

Say this aloud; *'With this, I burn everything that no longer serves me and I acknowledge the love that I am. Everything that has served me in purpose I embrace and have learned from it, I let my true inner self shine from now on. So be it'.*

Breathe and feel the lightness in you and smile. Smile because you know who you truly are.

Invocation
The unforgotten

You knew who I was,
even when I didn't know myself.
You saw the beauty in me and drew it out
so everyone can see who I truly am.
I see now who I am,
the light of the light, the heart,
the soul, the love.
The joy, the dance, the song,
the fire, the Goddess/God.
The eternal Beloved,
the loved one, the unforgotten,
I am a present to myself, and the world.
I am loved, I am loved.
I rejoice in this knowing.
I AM, I AM...I AM
My beloved, thank you, I love you.
Thank you, I love you.

CHAPTER NINE

RADIANCE OR COMING TO THE TRUTH

'So I wait for you like a lonely house till you will see me again and live in me. Till then my windows ache'.

Pablo Neruda, 100 Love Sonnets

"All you give is given to yourself"

Unknown author

Claiming your truth

When you enter the radiance stage it becomes a bit easier, it feels like you have climbed three quarters of the way up a mountain and you know that the peak is very near. You feel the excitement and you know in your heart that this journey is sacred.

By now, you are more confident and assured and you know the truth of this love. You have surrendered the outcome of this sacred relationship to Divine timing and the Divine way. You are free of attachment to the question of how and when it is going to manifest, you just know that it will. You completely trust in the intelligence of the Universe and its creativity.

The excitement comes from the knowledge that a surprise awaits you. At this point of the journey you claim your truth and are assured that you are having this experience and that it is valid for you. You stand strong in your truth no matter what.

You know the truth deep in your soul and your ego is gently integrated into your experience and is called to be of service to the Divine. It is not that your ego is not going to trick you anymore but now you are going to consciously observe it and you will not get caught up in it. You know that all the souls with whom you agreed to undertake this mission are going to benefit from this truth. As a twin soul you emanate this unconditional love which is all embracing.

This journey is beneficial for all involved, your soul mates, family, and children. It is so liberating to know that you do not need any validation of your experience from outside sources. As we accept our truth, we give permission to others around us to step into theirs as well. Now in the radiance stage when doubts raise their heads, it is even more essential not to give up. This is a stage of pure faith. For all of you who are not still reunited with your twin, now is the time to focus on yourself, do all the things that you want to do, take care of yourself, and nourish yourself. In the radiance stage, it is time to put your love into action and cultivate joy. This faith is the promise you have been given in your heart by the God/Goddess, and we all know that in the chambers of the heart there are no false promises. The promise is that you are going to achieve your embodied sacred Union, and through that unconditional love we will lead each other to a new earth. The heaven on earth will be where we will live this love.

You may or may not have 'proof' in the 3D for your Union, but still you believe in what you know to be true for you, and sometimes only you, because nobody else sees what is in your heart.

You are the holder of your fire, passion, and vision.

You are claiming your truth and everything that is false will go away. In the physical experience this may signify divorces or separations, meaning that relationships which are based on old beliefs will be ending. Also, you will be leaving jobs that drain your energy, and that give you no satisfaction, releasing old friends or any type of soul mate relationships that do not resonate with you any longer, and giving forgiveness to yourself and to everybody who hurt you in the past or present. You are going to be creating jobs that have a meaning for you or your purpose and that give you joy when you get up in the morning. Changing jobs and entering your heart's mission, letting go of everything that no longer serves your highest good. What is your highest good, you might be asking? This is different for everybody, because we do not all wish for the same outcomes. We are so unique and we all wish to express ourselves in a different way.

Your highest good is your best expression, the best version of yourself that you can be, it is you being free and singing your heart's song no matter what. This is you being in the presence of joy.

At this time of radiance on this stage of the journey, you are clearing lifetimes of clutter. To claim and own your truth means that you have to start making choices for you, out of love for yourself and not for the wrong reasons anymore, and trust that all of these choices are right for you. Actually, you are safe in the knowledge that you don't need anybody's permission anymore. All of that ego fear of the opinions of other people disappears. This doesn't mean that you don't respect people around you anymore, but rather you adhere to the notion that you respect your own integrity and your own truth, and let them live their own truth.

You are free to live your life the way your heart is guiding you to live it.

The big difference between this way of living and that of ego boundaries is that you do all of this with great love for everybody included. When you live your truth with integrity, it is beneficial to all, because it comes from the heart and soul. You bless and thank everybody in your life for being a part of your journey. Your life partner, your family or people close to you, might not be glad to see you stepping into your truth, because you are then showing them their own lie in the mirror, and some of them want to sleep a bit longer. Eventually they will understand that you are leading by example, and showing them how they could live from this place of authenticity too.

Bless them all and let them go, as everybody is as free as you are to believe in their own reality. Some of your soul agreements are over and you are moving on.

Be thankful for all of the lessons you learned, blessings you received from these relationships, and know that they were only the preparation for the ultimate relationship, the Union with your twin soul. Be thankful because all of these relationships prepared you, and they have prepared you well.

All that you went through was a preparation for the ultimate, and all of these relationships were sacred too and in the service of the Divine.

The charisma of radiance

The word *charisma* comes from the Greek word (kharizma) which means 'favour freely given' or a gift of 'grace'; charisma is compelling attractiveness or charm that can inspire devotion in others.

The charismatic person knows that they light the Divine spark just by being who they truly are, and people feel this authenticity. There is an aura of charisma about you from being in a phase of radiance and don't be too surprised when people are drawn to you unconsciously. Because you radiate this light people can feel your authenticity, even if they are not conscious of it.

You have heard people say so many times; 'there is something special about that person, but I just can't out a name on it'. People are going to be staring at you a lot, and sometimes it can get very funny. So many times, I thought I was wearing something hideous, until I realized it was the light that was drawing people, and then I just smiled and knew that it is the miracle of each of our lives to radiate this light. People often use this expression for somebody, saying; ' you've got something in you that I just can't put my finger on'. That something unnameable, indefinable, is charisma. That essence, that spark in you.

> *A charismatic person is the person who knows that he is the power force of the God/Goddess and that knowing emanates from his being.*

The charismatic person knows that they cannot lose in whatever they do, because they know you never lose, you just learn. They will use every 'failure' and turn it into success, meaning that they will absorb lessons faster and deeper than most people.
The irony of this phase is that you are going to have many people who are interested in you, but your heart is going to be open only for your twin. People around you will feel this magnetism in you because you radiate so much love, integrity and authenticity. If you are a true twin soul people will subconsciously feel this about you and be drawn to you.

> *To radiate love we do not have to physically do anything in the way we have been conditioned to think. You radiate love just the way you are because you embody and emanate from this higher frequency and this touches people who are in your presence.*

Charismatic people don't merely help others but rather they empower them to find the strength that they have lost in themselves. We all know that acts of 'altruism' are often a substitute for feeling good and are done for all the wrong motives like guilt, shame, or in order to feel good about yourself. The person who wants to help somebody may be doing so to reduce these 'bad' feelings in themselves and creates the illusion of being a 'good' person. We must be so aware, clear, and honest with ourselves about why we are doing something philanthropic.

A truly charismatic person is one who has self-love and a pure motive for wanting to help the other person see his or her own worth. In other words if you are helping somebody just to feel better about yourself this is not help at all. Think about this. Experiment and learn a bit more if you need to, maybe just to confirm to yourself that you have changed or that you don't have an interest in soul mate relationships any more, or gain some more insight into life. It is all well, whatever you choose. Some people choose to stay alone and experience the journey through this perspective.

Remember that even when you are in a relationship with another soul mate you will always keep the space in your heart for your twin. You can play out as many scenarios as you want until you choose differently. When you become conscious, you cannot just be, or stay with a partner who chooses to stay unconscious, because their choice is to sleep, and you are conscious and awake.

Your vibrations will just not match, because you will see everything from another perspective. That does not mean you do not love your partner or think that you are better in any way, but rather that you are aware of how much they helped you evolve, and now you need another challenge for evolving some more. This way you hold this gratitude in your heart for your soul mate partner, and for everybody else you decided to release.

To be able to understand that you can love in complete freedom and that love is not restricted to the physical presence, you need spiritual maturity.

At this point of the journey you may wish to try to meet someone new and different to fulfil you and give you something that is missing from your life but it is impossible for somebody to complete you as a person, you must first complete yourself. This is the old paradigm withdrawing from you, now that you consciously know that all fulfilment is firstly in yourself, and when you achieve this, the world will reflect to you, your own beauty and balance.

You start to think deeply what your mission is, and what is your heart's calling. You cannot be satisfied anymore acting like a robot on autopilot and living on survival mode in the world. Now, you are this powerful, conscious, aware human being who knows their creative achievements intimately, and knows that everything happens for you and not to you. Mastery, yes, this is mastery. The Universe is saying to you now; 'your wish is my command'.

Know this and take action toward your dreams. Go and sing your song like the birds do, not caring who listens; they just sing for the joy of it.

Singing your song

There is a saying from one of my favourite poets, Rumi, which is; *"I am going to sing my song no matter who listens or not"*. It is so beautiful to express yourself just for the sake of expression, for the sheer joy it gives you. You don't think about who is going to listen and what they are going to say or do with your song, you just sing because it makes you happy and it makes you more of who you are.

Yes, it is very important to fulfil your soul first. It is time to get off this wheel of karma and know that you are going to graduate from this earth school. You are going to enter your truth more and more every day, and start to feel the complete joy of living free from attaching yourself to your emotions and your life story. You are going to be a pure observer, and feel the power you have.

The joy of living when there is nothing outside of you that you are relying on to fulfil you gives you this feeling of ultimate freedom that you bestow on yourself and on others.

Your heart, maybe for the first time, is feeling the peace of balance, with the feminine and the masculine being in complete harmony, the masculine and the feminine in an embrace dancing to the rhythm of your soul. Express yourself and make this creation become more of who it is through you.

A beautiful thing to realise is that the creation would not be the same without you singing your song.

So sing it and do not care who listens or not.

The joy of living

We get to know the joy of living in this beautiful life by the breath streaming through us each second, and by trusting that we are loved and taken care of always. As we breathe we are nourished, from the ether of Divine food.

Jesus said; "Man shall not live on bread alone but on every word that comes from the mouth of God". We do not live only from food; we are also nourished from Divine 'food', which we are given through our spirit in each second of our lives.

The only thing left to do is to dance to the music of our souls in this great journey we call life, and to affect everybody with this divine rhythm. Let us just be aware of what a gift this life is and wake up from this dream of suffering. We are the kings and queens we have been searching for in the kingdom of love. Now let us act as such.

Meditation
Radiating love from your sacred heart

The purpose of this meditation is knowing that the love you have in your heart can affect the whole of humanity. This meditation is about coming into the heart and radiating that truth and light on everybody and everything that you see. It is acknowledging that you are this powerful human vessel radiating love.

By now, you know that you are a co-creator with the Divine to accomplish the mission of your heart.

In this twin soul mission, you are like a hero on a quest, and the only way you can come home is if you follow your own soul.

Sit or lie down, whichever feels more comfortable. Close your eyes, relax and breathe a few deep breaths to release tension and relax some more.

Put your hands on your heart and say this out loud; *'With this meditation I open my heart centre and allow the love to radiate onto everything and everybody that comes my way, and with this love I bless everybody and everything'.*

Now close your eyes and in your third eye see your heart pulsating inside your chest, feel the warmth of your heart, hear the heartbeat of life in sync with the breath of life. Feel how you are cared for with this heartbeat and this breath, and know that it is enough. There is peace in this knowing. Listen to your heart and the message it has for you. Call your twin forth so that they may be in your heart awareness as you open your heart. Now see the beautiful magenta light radiate from your heart, pouring out and embracing all. You see your heart opening like a beautiful flower. Firstly this light spreads from your heart all over your body, then onto the room, then onto the building you are in, then into the city where you live, the state, the continent, the planet. Allow it to travel to other galaxies and planets, as there are no boundaries.

Say this aloud; *'I bless all beings with this unconditional love'.* Feel the heart's expansion and opening. Feel the power to radiate this love to whomever you choose. Feel the freedom of this unconditional love which can nourish the whole, because it is so complete.

Stay in this blissful feeling for a while and when you have had sufficient time, open your eyes. Each time you do this meditation you are opening your heart and helping yourself to love unconditionally. Know that by doing this you are elevating your own vibration as well the vibration of the whole planet.

Be thankful that you can create in this loving way.

Invocation
Free to shine

We are free as the wind, flowing like the rivers of the world.
Warm like the sun, free to enter our hearts.
Free to dance and be happy,
To become whole, to close the circle of love.
To shine as bright as the stars,
 because we are one of them.
We are stardust pretending to be human,
 in this game of forever, playing, and playing some more....
Remembering our origins, we see clearly that we are free.
Forever we were free, freedom is ours to have and to know.
To create from that flow,
from that freedom, from that joy.
We are here to expand and shine brightly.
To let our light shine and radiate,
to light the Earth with this shine.

CHAPTER TEN

HARMONIZING OR COMING TO THE SELF

' I seem to have loved you in numberless forms, numberless times...In life after life, in age after age, forever. My spellbound heart has made and remade the necklace of songs, that you take as a gift, wear round your neck in your many forms, in life after life, in age after age, forever '.

Tagore, Endless love

*"Remember the entrance
to the sanctuary is inside you"*

Rumi

Balancing the polarities

Twin flames have the same soul frequency but are polar opposites; the feminine and masculine polarity. We all have the feminine and the masculine charge inside ourselves. This polarity does not have anything to do with gender, but rather with our expression of masculine and feminine qualities. When twins are together and interacting with each other it resembles two magnets, and when the polarities are balanced the twins are united and when they are out of this balance, they come apart.

They are like two human magnets forever attracting and repelling each other, until they realize what is going on in this dynamic. On the soul level, they feel this pull, and it manifests as a strong desire or a need to be near their twin. It feels like an overwhelming need to share, learn, and grow with their twin.

No matter where they are physically, the pull does not disappear. You may be continents or countries apart and it doesn't make a difference.

You must understand that the twin soul union is primarily a deep soul connection, and then the connection is on all other levels, but the deepest soul desire is where it first starts from.

The complete human being will be reborn when we embrace the two halves of the male and the female inside ourselves. No man is just a man and no woman is just a woman. We have traits of both genders and polarities within, including the more feminine ones such as gentleness, softness and nurturing, and giving, and the more masculine ones like strength, decisiveness, and action. The masculine needs to embrace the feminine in love, and vice versa, and this is first of all an internal process. In three dimensional reality this means integrating your truth and becoming the best possible version of yourself.

Do not strive for perfection from the ego standpoint but completely align from within what is true for you and express it. This means living your truth and following your heart, so that you can express your uniqueness in the world, because when you are balanced from within your both masculine and feminine qualities can express themselves in a completely new way. The question is; 'what is it that is calling you deep in your heart and waiting to be expressed for the benefit of the whole?'. This is the new balanced individual. The individual who has integrated the masculine and the feminine inside and from that space of wholeness he acts and brings peace into the world.

A complete human being has found the balance and maintains the equilibrium between masculine and feminine.

Feminine and masculine charge

At this point in time and earth ascension, I feel that we are starting to balance the two within ourselves, because we humans as a collective cannot function in this masculine-dominated society.

The conditioning goes very deep; men have been suppressed and cut off from the feminine aspect in them and women have been suppressed and cut off from their masculine aspect. All of this imbalance needs to be balanced again. Men who are more in touch with their feminine side cannot fully express themselves in this masculine-dominated society because they will immediately be labelled incompetent or too 'soft'.

In other words 'feminine' men tend to be ejected from the masculine 'tribe', and even to be ostracised.

A woman, on the other hand, who is in touch with her masculine side can be considered a threat to the average man and society, whether it be from her position in the family hierarchy, or in the wider worlds of the business and political arenas.

We must begin to understand that as human beings, we are neither completely feminine nor masculine, but rather within us we have both qualities overlapping and striving to find a balance together.

In contemporary society, women still struggle to find an equal footing with men in the workplace, in the family, and any arena where women and men are deemed to be in competition.

As a result of this imbalance, many women may strenuously strive to compete with men because they have been oppressed for so long. This energy of oppression can then become aggression where we see so many women trying to overcompensate and become 'men' and take a masculine role in society. I am not suggesting that women are incapable of achieving success in such roles but I would suggest that the wish for this has to come from a more balanced desire.

I believe that we are seeing so many wars, power games, and destructiveness in this world because we are all suppressed from one side of our polarity. Society has taught us to raise men to be cut off from their feminine side and women to be disconnected from their masculine energy, resulting in their powerlessness under the extreme expression of masculine energy. Women are raised to be submissive as though it is synonymous with being feminine.

In my opinion, this scenario is very far from the truth. Neither gender is still fully assimilated into their natural power. The woman of the future is going to stand in her own truth, strength, and wisdom while honouring her body as the sacred temple it is.

She is going to flow like water, in each moment accepting the flow of her feminine and masculine and knowing intuitively when to act, when to be calm and silent. The balanced woman knows who she is and what her nature is, but at the same time she does not feel threatened by a man, she loves and honours the man for who he is, and their best qualities interrelate in a divine relationship. She is the Goddess in her own right. She is beautiful, nurturing, supporting, but at the same time strong, decisive, and action orientated.

The new man is going to stand in his strength and power, with his intuition and wisdom honouring the woman for her gentleness, beauty, and strength. The man of the future is not going to feel threatened by her intuition and her power, he is going to be nourished by her abilities all the while embracing his intuitive and sensitive side. The man of the future is going to express his feelings openly, and be gentle and strong in a balanced way. The outer manifestations of the relationship will be only the reflection of the inner balance.

Every relationship is merely a reflection of where we are in our state of consciousness.

We have to see through this conditioning, and start to act differently as individuals. In addition, we must begin this process in our homes and families first, and raise our children in this freedom of expression regarding their emotions. We must be willing to raise this fresh generation of boys and girls in the new truth, and tell them that only together in harmony and respect can the feminine and masculine create heaven on earth. The energy is always neutral and ever flowing, it is we who give it the charge and the meaning. The feminine qualities are softness, nurturing, receiving. The feminine energy is like water flowing with ease. She is embracing, motherly, gentle, intuitive, sweet, and beautiful.

The masculine energy is very beautiful as well, supportive, comforting, decisive, strong, straightforward, and action orientated. The masculine energy is the giving energy. The masculine is comforting to the feminine and the feminine is comforting to the masculine. They need to embrace each other so that together they can thrive in this world. On this twin soul journey the embrace needs to happen from within and then the union can happen on the outside.

You cannot be in physical union with your ultimate soul partner until the unification and integration has first of all taken place inside of you. In all of our previous incarnations and journeys we were learning through soul mates how to bring these together.

We incarnated as both genders to get both perspectives, and now it is time for the merging of the two. Twin soul relationships are going to be the pioneers of the new model of balanced relationships, reinventing how we relate to each other and finding new ways of being.

When the masculine and feminine aspects are united inside of us there is nothing we need from anyone else to fulfil us. We feel balanced and complete and we are simply together to share the beauty of love and inspire others to do the same.

Just imagine the world where everybody is with their one true love. Oh, what a wonderful world this would be. I can see it in my spirit. I have imagined it and if you are reading this book, you probably have imagined it too. Through this experience of twin soul journey I see it is possible, and that is why we must trust ourselves. This love is not only about two individuals loving each other, through this love the divine performs its miracles. When you love yourself completely and at the same time you are as one with your twin, the only thing your heart wants is to pour this divine balm of love onto others.

In this balance you are neither masculine nor feminine, you are the fully embodied soul emerged in the heart completely. You transcend gender in a way.

In this balanced state, all the women of the world become your sisters, all of them become your mothers; they are the Divine expression in female form. In the same way all men become your brothers, fathers, sons, in the most intimate way because you realize the oneness of all. There is no need for repression of women, and there is no need for feminism either because both behaviours represent the two extremes. Men and women respect each other and take all of the beautiful qualities from each other. There is no more negative charge between the male and the female, there is no lust like in the old ways of sexual relating. There is no competition between genders but rather the passion of togetherness, the deep soul love like no other, where you feel you are whole and as if you are at home with your brothers and sisters. You see that men are the masculine expression of the Divine.

That is the true resurrection in my opinion, being in the body and knowing your divinity.

We do not have to have the experience of death anymore to be able to resurrect, we can have this Divine knowing while living in the body so that we can create miracles. My heart cries with joy when I see more and more people awakening to this truth, but I have to assure you that there are no shortcuts to your heart.
You must work your way through it, and there are as many ways as there are individual people. Some of the roads are going to lead you to your destination faster and some of the ways will be slower, but only when you sit with yourself and have an honest self-talk and decide that you are willing to do the work, will you succeed. In this journey of the heart you have to be willing to let go of everything you have been taught and embrace and create the new reality for yourself. The important thing is; *be honest with yourself. Be true to yourself.*

Holding in the middle of the infinity sign (enlightenment)

You are going to have to do the work first while at the same time discarding all that you have gathered along the way and staying calm and empty. This is the paradox of being enlightened. You may think that the enlightenment process has to do with gathering knowledge so that you can then enlighten.
Through my life experience this has proven not to be true; for me the process of enlightenment is the opposite, meaning that you have to unlearn and release everything you know and make space for the Divine to enter your being. You must understand that it does not matter what you do and what path you are taking to get

there, it only matters how willing you are to be empty and receptive. All of the knowledge you have learned and gathered is important but it is nothing compared to the truth of your soul.

Empty is not empty, because this emptiness is fullness at the same time, and thus it is a paradox. This emptiness teaches you what beauty is, it teaches you how to flow, it gives you the wisdom of the heart, it gives you strength, knowledge, action.

We can know something from the intellectual mind but knowledge needs to descend into the heart and integrate into the body. This means full integration, because we are mind, body, and soul.

Most people today operate only from their head (intellect), a smaller percentage use their heart consciously (intuition) and even a smaller percentage use their soul to guide them through life. As long as the knowledge is in your mind it is ok, if it is in your heart it is always beautiful and knowing, but when you fill your soul and body temple with this knowing, it is beyond happiness. Then we can say that we embody the knowledge fully.

When you integrate it feels as if you used to drive this slow old car, and now you have this Porsche and you can drive it to its full potential. The love is starting to pour from your cup and you need to share it, you do not mind who is going to drink from it but you know that whoever needs it the most is going to come. Holding in the middle of the infinity sign means being balanced, experiencing peace and calm.

On your way to enlighten when you start acknowledging how deeply you rejected yourself, it is going to hurt at first. This feels like you are calling your long lost child to come home, and you feel guilty, sad, and happy simultaneously. By accepting that hurt day by day you start to see the strength of love nourishing every lost aspect of you. You start to get softer and more vulnerable, you cry a lot, and that is ok because old blocks of energy are leaving the body from the cellular memory of this life and 'past' parallel lives.

> *We are like the observers of the one who has done and experienced everything, and this is called detachment, or observing from a higher perspective.*

It is like watching yourself in a movie where you are playing a leading role. As a past life regression therapist, working with my clients I saw first-hand that we as human beings can observe our experiences and be detached from them. When you observe yourself in a 'past life' you get a wider perspective of who you really are, a perspective of layers and layers of the richness of your inner being. In this eternal game we call life, we only observe minimal aspects of ourselves. This life here on Earth is only one aspect of us, and if we use the metaphor of a movie, your one role as a cowboy does not determine who you are in your totality as an actor. You can play as many roles in as many movies (parallel lives) as you want. You are just acting. If you have the capacity to observe yourself in 'past' lives, you have the ability to watch yourself in this one too. See clearly what role you are playing, what is the scenario of your current life, what is the theme you are enacting. Be conscious. Be aware.

In my own journey, on one occasion when my twin rejected me and I felt the pain, I saw clearly that I wanted this pain, which I was actually creating because this pain was on repeat mode and this situation had occurred so many times before. As he was rejecting me I was rejecting myself, until it hurt so much that that hurt slapped me in the face.

You don't see this clearly at the beginning of the connection until later on as you progress through the journey. I needed that pain so I could see clearly what a powerful creative being I am. In that moment of insight and revelation I saw that it is I who is doing this, he is only in service to me so I can see the truth. The feeling was almost like I was unconsciously testing whether he would reject me and for how long. Really, he was only showing me the mirror. This is how powerful this connection is. That was the last time I felt like a victim and afterwards I saw my own strength in full bloom.

Your twin is going to tell you that they do not want you because they want the purest and best version of you, they know this is possible even before you know it. They know you in your heart, they know your potential.

This is how powerful this love is. It transforms each twin so much. Loving ourselves is a process in which we must want to engage. We have been conditioned for so long to believe that loving ourselves is selfish, but it is absurd to even think that you can love anybody if you do not love yourself. How can you give what you do not have?

All of the relationships we had in the past with different soul mates have mostly been a substitute for the real rich experience of giving, out of self-love.

Women especially have been on this jaunt of giving out of sacrifice and not thinking about themselves, not thinking of nourishing themselves first. They were giving firstly by birthing children, then by nourishing and taking care of the family. A woman's body has been a gift to the earth and to hard toil, to her husband and to her family, but now it is time that women come back to themselves. By this men will gain so much as well in relating with women. Yes, to put your own needs first sometimes is at the core of fulfilling somebody else's needs. How can you give if you are frustrated and unfulfilled, if you are only left with crumbs? Instead of this selfless martyr archetype, a woman who cares about her needs is able to see freely the needs of other people around her and to act in love and from love. In your twin soul connection there is no stone left unturned, you have to be willing to go the extra mile for your twin. This connection asks of you to run this marathon and when you are completely exhausted, to run some more. This connection is only for the 'navy seals' of the marine corps of spirituality. Only the toughest will survive to see the finish line, only those who believe till the end.

In soul mate relationships, you can 'close your eyes' and decide not to look into yourself but in a twin soul connection you are 'forced' to look inside because the pull and the pain is so strong that you cannot look the other way.

This is the evidence that the love is always stronger than the fear and that is why you jump. The love is so strong that it feels like if you give up on this love it would feel the same as if you had 'died', because there is nothing else that can fulfil your heart on this earth but the notion of being true to yourself.
This journey shows you the truth so clearly. When you decide to continue after so many falls, it is difficult because there are so many challenges on this path. But when you awaken you know there is no way back, and you have to go on because now you cannot close your eyes and go back to 'sleep' again.

Loving yourself completely

In this journey to self-love there is beauty and in this self-love there is love for God/Goddess at the same time. We believed in this false rejected self for too long and the feeling of coming home is wonderful. Somebody once asked me how I can know love so intimately? I said; 'feel how you have never been separate from the Source, you have only been conditioned to believe so'.

Self-love is taking care of yourself, and loving every aspect of you, which has brought you to the knowledge of this person you are today. Loving yourself, in my understanding, is the clear comprehension of the false beliefs we had for so long about our 'fallen' self, and the acceptance of our divine self.

Self-love is the inner embrace of both shadow and light. The embrace and forgiveness of every mistake, failure, and ridiculous thing you did in your life because that brought you to this point of love. Forgiveness doesn't have much to do with external change but rather letting go inside of yourself of everything that hurt you in the past. Everything is necessary for our growth and that is beautiful.

Self-love is the essence of spiritual life and the truth is that we came into this world alone and will leave alone as well. When we 'exit' this plane of existence it is the only trip we ever take when we cannot take somebody with us.

Self-love is not selfish and does not exclude God/Goddess and people in your life but on the contrary, it includes God/Goddess and all.

In existentialist terms, we live primarily for our own experience and expansion, and then altruistically for others by the sharing of life experiences and mutual growth. Self-love is not selfish, but essential if we want to live a fulfilled life.

As long as are you projecting onto another and you have not looked into yourself you are not aligned with the highest truth, and you cannot possibly give something that you do not feel for yourself. We can only give and share with others what we have given first to ourselves.

That is the greatest love of all, coming home to your true self, your divine nature and finding the lost child within. Giving this child all the freedom to express, love and be happy about life.

Meditation
Healing the body with your twin

The purpose of this meditation is the healing of trauma that resides in your body. Our bodies have a memory and we can hold trauma and old energy in the body for a long time. We usually focus on the spirit and mind when we do healing but the body is as important. This healing meditation came to me when I was in my surrender stage during a time when a big portion of healing and inner work happened.

In this sacred journey, you always are becoming more of your true self. It is an eternal, beautiful, ever evolving journey, and there is no goal to reach in this worldly view but rather with each step you take, you are stepping evermore into the light of your own soul. Moreover, this spiritual path is different for all of us, because we are so unique.

Find some quiet place where you will not be disturbed and where you can relax, lie down, or sit, as you prefer. Close your eyes and allow your awareness to focus on your breath. Breathe deeply a couple of times to release any tension from the body. With every breath you take, you feel calmer and more relaxed. Your breath massages your inner being and all of your organs.

See with your inner eye and vision, a room or a safe place of comfort and peace. You are lying on the bed and feeling cosy, warm, safe, and loved. Lying beside you is your beloved, you are so happy and feel as though nothing is missing in this world or that nothing could be added to this moment. You feel completely surrounded with love and warmth.

As you experience the love you start to tell your twin about your body, where you store your tension, trauma, where you feel the pain, and most importantly, where your guilt and shame are located. You tell your twin to put their hands on every part that needs releasing and healing.

Every true twin soul is a natural born healer even if they are not aware of it or practice it.

As they go through and 'scan' your body energy, feel the love washing it all away and melting all that you no longer need for your growth. See all that tension, guilt, and shame that you stored in your body coming out in the form of grey smoke. It is happening right now, as you are doing this healing, healing does not have to take time, we just need to allow it at this very moment. Whatever emotion you feel, let it out of your body. You can cry if you need to, talk to your twin about how you feel or do whatever comes to you naturally. This healing meditation has a tremendous power because you are doing it with your twin so the energy is doubled and elevated for healing to take place. You are a powerful force of love. Know that. Affirm this to yourself; *'My body is a sacred, beautiful, strong, healthy temple of my soul. I love and accept my body completely. So be it'.*

With your love you can create anything in the moment. You create a third energy that is very powerful and send it into the ether for the world to breathe. This energy is so true, so beautiful and you can feel it as your body becomes lighter and lighter. When you feel you have had enough time you can repeat the process on your twin as well. You can see the white golden light moving through your body from your toes to the top of your head and from the top of your head to your toes. If you feel you are ashamed of your twin that means you are ashamed of yourself, so accept yourself totally. Feel any sensation that comes to you and share it with your twin.

All of your beautiful imperfections are what make you exactly who you are. When you feel you have had enough, thank your twin and open your eyes.

Know that your body is a temple of love where the Divine resides. Be grateful for your body.

Invocation
I see clearly

Your body soul is the Holy Grail I have to find,
to become whole, to understand completion.
To break the illusion of the flesh,
 because we are soul wearing the flesh
 not the flesh wearing the soul.
We are dancing in this world for a while
and trying to capture the truth,
but truth cannot be found in searching only.
It is found when we see it has been in us all along.
I see you clearly my Beloved,
You helped to remove the veils, my love.
Now I see the light of all, reflecting through me.
I see the light of me, reflecting through all.
I see us in this beauty, sharing our gifts
with all of existence.
Our bodies don't exist anymore, we are lost and
see nothing but the soul.
There are no borders between the whole and our bodies.
Who are we in this bliss, I ask you?
We are all, you say to me and you kiss me.
In this kiss, I feel the whole world beating inside of me.

CHAPTER ELEVEN

THE LESSONS OF THIS CONNECTION

' A twin soul is not found. A twin soul is recognized '.

Vironika Tugaleva

' Everything we need is given to us and everything we need to know is revealed to us'.

Bible

Your core experience

Through this sacred connection, you are going to become aware of what your core experience is here on earth. There is one core experience which is universal to all twin souls, and that is coming to the self, or into Union within.

The main purpose of the twin soul journey is coming into Christ's consciousness.

This is the number one task, to embody this union within ;'as above so it is below', meaning that all of your being is integrated into one spark of love.

Coming 'into the self' means knowing yourself well and loving yourself out of that knowing.

Your personal core experience might be that you have to learn how to forgive, how to be strong, maybe you came here to know what it is to be gentle, or passionate and so on, but you will feel like there is one predominant theme going on in your life.

Every spiritual journey has a theme of learning; I am not saying there's only one because we learn many things through life, but one that is more persistent and more obvious than the others. In my personal experience, my twin soul journey, among other lessons, taught me how to be strong and independent. You will feel the dominant theme emerging, for example, you might feel that forgiveness is very important for you but learning how to be gentle, perhaps, is not so essential and does not have such a charge. Through the twin soul journey you will feel and know what your main theme is. Through this core experience, you change, evolve, and understand yourself better and ultimately you become more of who you really are. Your twin soul journey finally gives you clarity about who you are; it is like looking into a clear reflection of yourself in the mirror.

Even though you were reluctant to look at yourself in this mirror, in the end you understood that if you did not look you would miss seeing this great person, this beautiful human being who deserves only the best.

Be thankful to your twin for mirroring this beauty to you. It was not easy for them either while they were holding the mirror for you to see your reflection. Remember that you are one and when it was hard for you, it was hard for them too.

Be thankful for all the rejection, the pain, the tears, as on the way they made you shine like a diamond. You were a diamond in the rough and your twin did not want to give up on you until he saw you shine. Thank your twin for this journey because you did this together. Now you can shine your light into the world.

The interdependence of all life

This core learning is going to become increasingly clearer until you completely integrate what you have learned. You are by now aware that all life is interdependent and fused into one sea of consciousness.

You are not one separate entity floating through the universe but rather a beautiful spark of Source, God/Goddess, coming together with other beautiful sparks, and creating that unified field of one love.

As we descended into this dense three dimensional reality (that is this world) we believed for so long that this is all, searching for the Divine in all the wrong places, wandering and roaming the earth, asking ourselves for the meaning of our existence.

In this time of awakening of consciousness, we see clearly what our potential is, firstly as individuals, and then collectively. We as humans today are blessed to witness these changes, and we can place the seeds of love into our hearts to wish for a different earth experience ,one which will become true if we all wish for it. Most of all we should cultivate compassion in our hearts so that we can understand those who are suffering still and give hope to each other for a better, new way of living. I imagine this new way of living every day and I am happy to know many of us are imagining the same.

Many people are waking up to this new reality; *"Imagine all the people living life in peace... you may say I'm a dreamer but I am not the only one..."* said John Lennon in 'Imagine', his legendary hymn to peace.

Integrating all of your experiences

You are going to experience all of your roles in 'past' lives and see that they are just a play on the screen of consciousness. As your body becomes less dense, you start to have visions of your 'past lives' and present life merging because time as linear ceases to exist for you anymore.

You live all your multidimensional lives at the same time with this life reality and you know what you are feeling. You are integrating all of these experiences so that they can come into a single focus for your best growth. From different timelines in multiple dimensions you are bringing all the important pieces into this current timeline so you can gain all the wisdom for ascending in this lifetime.

'Past life' talents are coming through to be integrated into this experience. This serves the purpose of integrating all of your experiences so that you can enter a fifth dimensional reality of being, where the rules of the three dimensional reality do not apply anymore. When integrating, you are going to feel the density of your physical body and many symptoms of creating the *Merkaba* (light body) which is less dense. The body structure of a stone is not the same as that of a feather. This time you wished for yourself to be lighter and express yourself lightly. Integration is not an easy process because you have to shed everything of lower vibration so that you can make space for higher vibration reality.

Your whole physical body has to adjust to this process. This integration or the ascension process can be extremely painful and very challenging before you can emerge as 'lighter'.

We tend to perceive reality as a concrete, solid space-time but reality is rather as flowing as the individual perceives it to be.

We come in and out of so many realities in one day. As I write this book, I have in front of me a beautiful figure of two angels in an embrace, holding a red heart between their hands. That is the twin soul and heart connection, in which both you and your twin soul hold one heart, meaning that you are coming into awareness that you are one. All your life experiences are going to seem like they are coming into one and you see a purpose in each one of them. There is a common thread in all of them, a thread that connects all of your experiences. You see that everything was needed, in your journey.

You understand and see some things that happened in your past clearly, and what the purpose was of them. Embrace all of your experiences. My heart is experiencing so much joy in this moment of sharing with you my reader, and I hope that with the energy of my heart I will be able to touch your heart.

I know this is so, and my hope is that one day as a human race we are going to look at each other and communicate through our hearts. I know that our hearts will lead and that we will not need words so much, because we will be so sensitive to feeling. When you integrate yourself, sometimes there are no words needed because the energy flows and in this journey, your twin is here to show you that you are a telepathic being able to communicate no matter the distance. Integrating all of the knowledge into the body means you will go through some pain, you are going to feel all kinds of aches and discomfort in the parts of the physical and emotional body where the cellular memory is held.

Releasing particular memories is going to hurt, because these memories have been there for too long. You are going to feel disorientated. This integration process is not easy and when you are in the middle of it, you are going to feel something similar to depression because you have left behind the old three-dimensional model of relating and everything feels like it is coming apart. The new fifth dimensional reality is still not visible, so you will feel like you have been left hanging there in between what you knew and what's to come. However, you have to have faith and hang on. Awakening to a new reality is a process and while it was good to sleep and to play that game of not knowing, nothing can compare to the truth and the freedom of your inner being. Go for this awakening journey and do not give up just before the finish line. Even when it seems nothing is going on, trust me it is.

When nothing is going on in the external, it is actually a sign that a miracle is just around the corner.

Now breathe and smile because you deserve it. Smile and nourish your soul, and love your heart because you have been through it all, all of the turmoil and heartbreak so you can see how beautiful you are. You are beautiful, know that, and you are going 'home'.

One love

In this sweet awakening to the power of who we are, we are willing to go deeper and deeper until our false identity is seen for what it is and only the Divine is left. Each one of us who is awakened into the heart consciousness is bringing forth One love for this planet because we are One ocean of consciousness. One love, for all of humanity, that is all we need as a human race. From that love and oneness a peace will come, a peace which honours all life on this planet. Know that even if you have no communication in the 3D with your twin you can still complete integration. This is an internal process, and you communicate with your twin in your heart all the time.
When we create something at first we create everything in our imaginations and then it is only a matter of time until you see them manifested in this three dimensional reality.

The ultimate faith is to believe first and then to see, instead of the old three-dimensional paradigm of seeing it first and then believing it.

Know what you know. Own your knowing. Contemplate with the highest awareness on this; you know what you know, and it is enough. You are enough. You trusted so many for so long; your parents, friends, siblings, neighbours, religion, school, the system; it is time now to trust yourself. Amen to that.

Meditation
Meet your higher self

The purpose of this meditation is to meet your higher self, of which you are an extension. Your higher self is you at the peak of your potential, your best version, so to speak. You can get guidance from your higher self for healing, purpose, and insight.
 Your higher self is always waiting to fulfil your wishes for your expansion and is there to say; 'your wish is my command'. Every aspect of your psyche expands through your desire to become more, and out of the sea of possibilities, your higher self is that best possible version of your expansion.

Find a place where you will not be disturbed for half an hour. Create an atmosphere of peace and calm. Lie down or sit down, whatever you prefer. Relax your body and breathe. Start to observe and listen to your breath as it goes in and out of your nose. Feel the life force flowing through you. With every breath you take, you are more and more relaxed.
 Now say aloud ;*'I am ready and eager to meet my higher self for my highest possible good and expansion'*. Breathe and relax more deeply with every breath.
 In your inner vision, see a beautiful garden in springtime, all the nature is bursting with abundance. Smell the scents coming from all around you, feel the sun on your face. You are feeling calm, relaxed, and safe. You see a bench and you sit there. See all the beautiful colours of the landscape, green, pink, white, yellow glowing in this day. In the distance, you see a figure approaching you and it is your higher self. Allow whatever comes to you, see, and look with no censoring. Your higher self can manifest in any form which is recognizable to you, or which resonates with you. Your higher self represents your best possible version of who you truly are in reality.

Your higher self loves you unconditionally and wants you to express yourself from this love. Now you can ask your higher self a question or anything else about your life, your twin soul, your purpose, anything you wish. Ask and be still, and listen. Listen with your heart, listen with all the beauty in you. Feel this version of you come alive and evident for all to see. Feel this power of love and infinite abundance.

Relax and enjoy for a while. You can write down your insights if you wish to. When you have had enough time, open your eyes.

Whenever you feel the need for advice, you can come to this garden and call your higher self. Knowing this you can connect to the higher self of your beloved and help each other. Everything is unfolding in a beautiful and peaceful way. Trust this journey and relax. All is well.

Invocation
The gift of love

We reflect each other
 as the moon reflects onto the river,
we reflect because we are one, my Beloved.
One we are, all of us one humanity.
The grid of life is waiting for us
 to give this love to all existence.
We know we can do it, we know who we are.
The children of the Divine manifested into form.
We can do it my love, for all,
 let this love be a gift to all.
We can do it together,
like one breath of God/Goddess,
like one dream of God/Goddess.
It is the best imagining of this love the Divine ever had.
We manifest like the true kings and queens of life.
We see this now. We believe it now. We do it now. We receive it now.

CHAPTER TWELVE

THE MISSION

'I am longing to be with you, and by the sea, where we can talk together freely and build our castles in the air'.

Bram Stoker, Dracula

The one thing that you have that nobody has is YOU YOUR voice YOUR mind YOUR story YOUR vision. So write and draw and build and play and sing and dance and live as only YOU can.

Unknown author

Giving this love to the world

This soul love is going to push you towards your mission and your true heart's desire. You were born to change everyone who is in proximity to you, with this love. You are a walking generator of love who goes forth and affects the vibrations of others. This mission doesn't have to be 'important' from the worldly perspective of ego, but you will feel that from now on whatever you do you are doing it for this Divine love. The smallest tasks of the day are going to be executed with love and as an offering to the Divine.

There is not such a small task that it does not contribute to the whole, and there is nowhere where God/Goddess is not.

An unimportant 'job' doesn't exist, even the fluttering of the butterfly's wings can affect the hurricane on the other side of the world. Even one look and one smile can make somebody's day, one word said at the right time can change somebody's life, even one movement out of love is felt in this world and can affect others. We are all on a mission, but the mission I am talking about is for those who feel they are 'called' to do something. It is a calling from the inside, so strong that you feel compelled to do something. This calling in you demonstrates your deepest heart's desire, it shows you what you came to do or to change here on earth. This calling shows you what you have to share with others.

The deep soul love you feel for your twin creates a third energy, a very potent love, which propels you to spread it to the whole world, and this love is going to help elevate the vibration of the whole planet.

This soul love transcends the love between two people and shows you the love of God/Goddess. Twin souls have a mission together causing their talents to elevate when they are with each other, and in this way they can influence many people. Their talents complete each other. They reinforce each other so that they can create in a brilliant way.

Twin souls have a specific mission to fulfil together, which can manifest in any field of work, but the main characteristic is that it will affect many, and change the status quo. So go on; write that book, paint from the heart, open that shop, work for justice in the world. It doesn't have to be an artistic or a healing profession but whatever you do, make the world a better place.

One person who holds the vibration of unconditional love can help to elevate the vibration of 750,000 others who are not conscious during a lifetime. That is how powerful you are. Be that force of love. Be the change you wish to see in the world.

It is not about you

This mission is not about you, this mission is not a goal that is going to benefit only you. This calling you are going to fulfil is for the benefit of not only yourself but others as well.

The mission always touches other lives, because it is the God/Goddess creating through you. You are being a vessel for this Divine love to come and heal, change, inspire, show people that it can be different.

The mission always involves a vision you see in your heart, usually involving a condition which you want to elevate, change, or make better for all and through that calling you want to help it come to life.

It does not matter what kind of job you do, every job is as important as the next. In every job we perform we serve somebody. What is important is that you appreciate what you do and serve people with love. When that happens, then this wave of love is going to spread with no end in sight.

Martin Luther King said; *"Even if it falls your lot to be a street sweeper go on out and sweep streets like Michelangelo painted pictures. Sweep streets like Handel and Beethoven composed music, sweep streets like Shakespeare wrote poetry; sweep streets so well that all the host of heaven and earth will have to pause and say; 'Here lived a great street sweeper who did his job well' "*

We all have an individual mission, and no matter what job you do, your mission is to always give somebody the best service. You can touch lives whether you work in the bank or in a coffee shop. Make the best coffee somebody ever had, clean the street as if it is a royal palace, or if you are a healer show somebody the way that they can heal themselves. All jobs in the world serve, through work we serve

each other. In the eyes of the divine, all jobs are the same because God/Goddess sees that you are doing the best you can, from your heart, from wherever you are at that moment. As twin souls start to come together, they are going to raise the vibration of the earth with their love in action. Imagine them like sparkles of fire coming together, making a bigger fire, and with this fire, burning everything that is not true and lighting up the world. No man would ever go to war if he loved himself and his twin soul.
I guarantee you that. Imagine twin souls in this Divine love changing the existing vibration on earth, so that everybody can see that love is real and that love can create miracles. Through embodying love the world would change completely, and in the future, it will for sure. My highest hope and wish is to see this change manifested.

Love wave

The 'love wave' is here whether we feel it or not. The only question is whether you are going to be ready and willing to ride it. Our beautiful planet Earth is receiving boosts of energy from the Universe all the time at this point of ascension and shift. We are not left alone here on earth and we have helpers from other dimensional realities and intelligent races from other galaxies. There have been a few waves of energy portals opened over these past years, and every living creature on this planet was touched by these energies, even if they were not conscious of them.
The planet earth as a living organism is raising in vibration also. These love waves as I like to call them, will be washing over us until we are awake.
These waves come from the whole Universe and other galaxies, to help us rise to the task of creating a vibrational shift on Earth. Be aware that we are going to do it; we are doing it one by one.

Gandhi's saying; *"Be the change you wish to see in the world "* never rang more true than now for each one of us. If we don't shift our perspective on life and start to live with more love and compassion we are going to destroy the planet and the life form as we know it now. Who are we expecting to execute this change, if we are not going to do it? Who are we waiting for?

We are the ones we have been waiting for. It has always been us. Let us move on then, and do it. We do it by each one of us entering our hearts and being willing to live life from that higher awareness. This will be the second coming of Christ (consciousness) on earth.

Higher frequency on earth

The planet we live on is a live being; our planet Earth is energetically like a mother who keeps us in her embrace, and at this moment has a certain frequency. This frequency of the earth is constantly rising, while our frequency is rising as well, so that we can perceive a higher vibration reality. We are one with this earth, so we cannot perceive her as separate any more.

We humans have a certain frequency so we can perceive this reality and as we change and elevate this frequency, our perception of reality changes as well.

Her woods and trees are our lungs, her rivers, seas represent our veins and blood, her soils full of life and beautiful food are in service to our nourishment and life. As we breathe, she breathes as well.

Our own birthing of ideas in our abundant souls is the same as her abundant soil full of rich food for our bodies and our survival. When she is full of love and abundance for us, we are also full of love and compassion, because we feel that we are fed, and

nourished. Humans have treated her with no respect for so long and thus she is only reflecting our own state of being, which is out of alignment with the highest vibration of love. Human beings are the only species on earth who do not live in harmony with nature. Earth is reflecting our own vibration of hate, anger, greed, with the destruction caused by floods, tornadoes, and earthquakes. Floods and earthquakes are a vibrational imbalance of our planet, and the earth discharges these imbalances this way.
This imbalance is like a cancer cell on a part of Earth's body. It is comparable to the human body needing a cleansing process of its system for the purpose of bringing the balance back. In this journey of life we have a collective mission to restore life on earth and to live in peace and harmony with all human beings and all forms of life. There is so much abundance for all of us on this planet if we could only open our eyes and truly see. We need to become a collaborative society and stop this competitive madness.

If we start to collaborate instead of compete, in this way we can all strive and show our best talents and skills, this way all our talents complement each other and make progress much faster than when we compete with each other.

Einstein once said: *"If you judge a fish by its ability to climb a tree, it will live its whole life believing that it is stupid"*. The present model of the educational system needs to be completely reinvented in the years to come.

We are all in the service of each other. Serve, that is all, serve the best you can in the moment that you do it. The rest will take care of itself.

Only the ego compares and makes one person more important than another and while this world functions by competing, we must come into awareness that only by coming together and cooperating are we going to create a new Earth of equality and peace. We must come to the awareness that we are one, and that we need each other to complete all of the parts of the divine puzzle.

When you find your heart, your mission is going to become apparent.

You are not going to be called to do something you wished for yourself from an egotistical stance, but rather you are going to be 'placed' where you are needed most so that your talents can be used to the greatest advantage for the benefit of all. We have all been given talents so that we can share them and we should have no limits in sharing them.

When you unite inside, the natural urge that comes from the state of knowing your mission is to share what you know with others.

There are always going to be lots of people who resonate with what you have to give. From your truth and sharing they can flow and raise in their awareness. What one of us knows benefits all of us. For those who don't resonate with your truth and are negative (denying the Divine in them), leave them in peace and pray for them that one day they have the courage to enter and love their hearts too. A negative person is just one who still hasn't begun to love their hearts yet. You as a conscious human being are not here to energetically play games of the ego with them, or to show them what is right from your ego view point but rather you are here to be compassionate and see their struggle in accepting their hearts.

A negative person, as the word itself implies is negating life, negativity means that you have shut off the flow of life through you.

Do not forget that you were once there. The only thing you have to do is stand in your own heart truth. There is nothing that a negative person can take from you if you do not allow it. If the negativity affects you so much that you get caught up in the drama it means that you are still not anchored in your heart.

Remember that love is the strongest vibration in the universe and nothing can make it less.

You are very vulnerable when you love, but it doesn't matter, be open anyway to everything that wants to come your way. Usually we think that vulnerability is going to attract people who will 'use' us in life but this is far from the truth. Love is a shield that keeps you from negativity. You shield yourself only with love, you are a walking light, and every negative thing goes blind in your presence. So yes, my advice is, become vulnerable so that your heart cracks open and become humble, be soft, open to receiving, gentle, and full of beauty. In this twin soul journey your heart has been broken and kicked so many times that in the end it had to fully open. Only a broken heart can become fully receptive, a heart that protects itself might be 'safe' but in that false safety you would never know what your heart might gain, you would never even get to taste the real love. That is why your beloved 'broke' your heart, so that more light can enter, that is how much they love you. They want to see the best of the best in you. Even if that means that the methods your twin is using are a bit 'brutal', even then you know that your twin loves you. What you might gain is beyond the wildest imagination of the ego. When you think something from the ego perspective that thinking is always going to be somehow restricted. When doubts come, the lower feelings start to emerge and you feel limited. But when we have a vision from our heart, this vision is unlimited and there is no doubt, because it has a very strong soul signature.

The doubt always comes from the ego not from our soul.

Twin soul journey is beautiful and cruel at the same time, because the Divine wants to straighten you up like a strict parent who wants the best for you, but you know that throughout this process you are loved. Throughout this twin soul journey we are tested time after time, but watched over with so much love and care. We are the Divine children and we must not forget that. We are not here at this time and place by accident, we consciously chose to come here and be Earth angels. So many twin souls are going to awaken for Earth in these next couple of years. So now, there is no going back to the old, even if it hurts very much and you cannot see the outcome of this journey. This journey is coming all the way to its completion.

All the promises are written in the stars, where we came from.

This completion and coming home is our inheritance and our birthright.

All of this heart knowing knowledge, is going to be the inheritance we leave to our children. I think that is the best inheritance that they could wish for. Imagine many twin soul couples spreading the unconditional love they learned from this journey onto Earth and elevating the present situation. You are very much needed, each one of you.

Meditation
Guardian angels of guidance and healing

The purpose of this meditation is to connect you to your inner guidance. All of us here on earth are not left alone or cut off from Source. We have our inner navigational system, only if we are willing to open our inner ears and eyes, and truly listen and see.

This meditation is about a higher guidance we receive daily in our lives. It does not matter what Higher power you believe in; God/Goddess, Jesus, Mary, Buddha, Brahman, angels, spiritual guides, beings of light, Ascended masters; the important thing is that regardless of what religion you practice we are all helped along this journey on this planet.

We are never left alone, know that for sure. In this meditation, you are going to call your guardian angels for your soul purpose. When we connect to our Divine helpers, it is much easier to flow through our life.

Lie down or sit somewhere where you will not be disturbed for half an hour. Breathe and feel your breath coming in and out of your body. With every breath, you are feeling more and more relaxed. Imagine yourself sitting on a beautiful beach under a tree, completely relaxed and at peace. Smell the salt in the air, see the clear crystal blue sea, feel the warm, soft sand under your feet. It is a beautiful sunny day and you feel the light breeze on your face. You feel comfortable and peaceful surrounded by this beautiful scenery.

See with your inner sight and vision your guardian angels approaching you, these are your two guardians given to you at the time of your birth and will be with you until the day you decide to leave this reality.

Feel the love, peace, warmth, security that comes from your angels. You can ask for their names if you wish. As you feel these beautiful feelings from your angels, you are healing at the same time, because angels are high vibration beings of pure light, and whenever you align yourself to feel, hear or see them, you are healing just by being in their presence.

Now you can ask your angels to show you clearly what your specific mission is for this lifetime, or you can tell them your heart desires and see what they say. You can talk to them and tell them your biggest pains, hurts and fears and they will give you insights on how to heal or release hurt. Stay with your angels as long as you need to, until you feel reassured and at peace. You can call your twin forth, so you both can be healed and blessed by your guardian angels.

Every time when you are in doubt about your mission or path, you can come to your angels in this beautiful meditation.

Say this aloud: *'My dear and beautiful guardian angels stay with me throughout my life, guide and help me become my highest version on earth'.*

Angels are so happy to be of assistance and there is no task too small for them, but at the same time, they respect your own free will and will not interfere by giving advice or help if you do not specifically ask. Angels are your personal helpers and guardians and this is how much these messengers of God love you. We each have been given two helpers here on Earth, and they are like our personal bodyguards. Listen with your inner ears and your heart and stay in truth. Notice what message you got in this meditation and if you feel like it, you can write it down. When you feel you have had enough time, thank your angels for this guidance, open your eyes and stay in this knowledge. Your guardian angels are always by your side.

Call them for help whenever you need them. They are smiling and rejoicing when you ask for guidance and assistance. They are smiling that you are remembering, and coming into the joy of your true self.

Invocation
My angel on earth

My Beloved, my heart and soul,
my prince, my king,
my angel on earth.
You are my eternal angel guiding me so I can
see who I can become.
We come together in recognition
of who we truly are.
We are the Divine expressing through form,
loving unconditionally, flowing easily.
Loving is easy like breathing for us,
oh my beloved.
This love flows and
our hearts ignite in this sacred fire.
Our angels kiss in Divine embrace;
they dance the dance of love and joy for us.
The angels witnessed this sacred love and smiled.
Be happy my love, for we are so loved.
Feel it, feel it my love.

CHAPTER THIRTEEN

EMANATION AND FORCE OF UNCONDITIONAL LOVE

' I wish I'd done everything on Earth with you '.

F. Scott Fitzgerald

"Intense, unconditional love does not measure, it just gives".

-Mother Teresa-

Changing the blood family template

ll true twin souls have a greater mission that they can even imagine.

Twin souls are the angelic beings who volunteered here on earth to help in every way to raise the vibration and clear the old patterns of conditioning and functioning.

They are here to change the whole template of the lineage of the blood (Earth) family into which they have chosen to incarnate. By being and living inside their family, they affect the family members by their energy and changes occur where karma is being cleared and new templates of relating to each other are being established. Twin souls are here to transmute the dysfunctional templates in their families and to clear ancestral bloodlines.

They change everything with this love and in doing so they let the people around them see what is repressed in them. They are the catalysts for change in their blood family and in this way they modify old templates.

Born empathic, as twin souls were aware of other peoples' energies and patterns from an early age. We always tried to make people feel better so that we did not have to absorb their pain.

Empaths regularly take on other peoples' feelings and confuse them with their own.

If you are a particularly sensitive empath you are likely a 'receiver' of peoples' negative energy. With your high vibration you can transmute their energy but you have to be constantly aware of where you are vibrationally. Many times when I was growing up I would unintentionally take on somebody else's suffering and it felt so heavy upon me until I understood what was going on.

Taking on the sufferings of others is something that empaths do on a regular basis and often it is not easy, because of the amount of souls involved in this journey.

This connection has such strength, and goes so far that even ancestral karma is 'revived' so that all of the lineage is complete. What a task for a pair of twins to take on, and it is so brave. Yes, we are brave. We just forgot that for a while.

Preparing the way for your children

The children of twin souls, including the children conceived from soul mate relationships, are mostly twin souls themselves and the energy of these children also assists the coming into Union.

Each generation of a blood family brings a new template but the twin souls lock the new in so that the old can transform. They act as the guardians of the love they brought and make sure that everything is in place. At this time of being here on earth, we are collectively clearing the karma, because nothing must stand in the way of the union of twin souls.

Many of our soul mate relationships will come to a natural conclusion and new karma-free soul families are going to be formed for the enhancement of all. You are going to feel that some people you knew for a long time do not vibrate with you anymore, and that is fine. These are all karmic relationships with people who are very familiar to you.

A karmic relationship is a relationship where we set in motion an issue from a 'previous life' to be revealed and dealt with. In a way all soul mate relationships are karmic, because we came 'back' with souls we know from 'before'.

You have to go with your feeling because you will have a physical reaction to some people. Honour yourself and them, and let them go in love when it is time. On this path of ascension, you are going to start to meet people from your soul family who have a mission together with you. You are going to recognize them in your soul and being, and be well acquainted with them even if you know them only for a very short time in this life. Everything will feel like it's turned upside down, and everything you thought you knew about how relationships function will change.

On this beautiful journey, we are preparing the way for our children and teaching them by example that only unconditional love can keep us near to Divinity.

We have to lead by example because children learn from what they see and not what you tell them. They are very observant and intelligent. They sense our core being and no mask can hide you when you are in the presence of children, especially in the presence of your own child. They are here to teach us to come back to our innocence and to live life true to ourselves. This is especially true of the new *rainbow and crystalline children* who were born with this new spiritual technology, which is embedded in their DNA.

We have to be very aware of everything they bring and be thankful for it. It is very challenging to live with these new children because they have x-ray eyes and can look through you and tell from your energy what your issues are or what you need to work on. They act as a constant reminder so that you do not go to sleep again. They push you to your core even though they are such adorable, sweet, light-bearers. They carry this truth around and observe you, until you are willing to let go in this game of resistance.

I have three beautiful children and I am so thankful for this journey of motherhood, and grateful for what they constantly teach me.

Parenthood is a beautiful, amazing adventure and at the same time most challenging and demanding journey, as all parents know. My children teach me every day the truth of living life with ease. They teach me that I am ok just the way I am. They teach me to love myself. They teach me to relax and enjoy every moment of life, to live life in the now, to surrender to love. Our children anchor us in our truth, and as much as we teach them, they teach us at the same time. Have you ever thought that your child might have lived a thousand lives and can teach you a great deal about how to live? We can teach our kids how to do practical things in life, like brush their teeth, cross the street and so on, but when it comes to the truths of experiencing life, an equal sharing and exchanging of information is happening. We are equals, so do not be tempted to underestimate your child because they may be an 'advanced soul' who can teach you a great deal. At this point on the planet we travel, learn, and absorb so fast that sometimes we begin to think we can't take in all of the information at this pace.

You have seen through your shadow, you have seen everything, and now this dichotomy is collapsing in front of your eyes. You begin to see through the veil of this game we call duality. We came here to experience this game of duality and to learn through contrast. How would you know what light is if you didn't have the dark? How would you know what fullness is without emptiness?

The Universe works through paradox, when we face the opposite of what we desire we know more of what we truly want.

If you incarnated on earth and wanted to know freedom, you would incarnate into the conditions that took that freedom away from you. That is called contrasting experience, which enables you to come into the knowing of the experience you wanted to learn. In the awakened state of being we see through this contrast, and know the oneness of all.

You leave this duality game of good and bad behind, and like a phoenix you rise above because we are the sky and all else is just clouds passing by. When we see through this game of duality we realize that this dichotomy only exists in this 3d reality; on higher planes of existence we are one and all of existence dances to the rhythm of love. Through duality and contrast, we learn and expand.

With every choice we make we expand. If we think from a higher perspective there are no wrong choices because we always become more than we were before.

Clearing the karma

A conscious human being cannot any longer create bad karma because he operates from a higher frequency of perceiving reality. Karma by definition means action, work or deed.

Karma means that every action creates a reaction, a cause and effect. The intent and actions (cause) influence the future of that individual (effect).

Therefore, we create karma as we live each second of our lives with our intent and actions. I do not like to look at karma as something set in stone or some kind of a static form of 'punishment'. I rather see it as a dance between cause and effect where we can influence both and clear it along the way, a flowing change of circumstances where you have the awareness to shape every second. Karma can manifest instantly or over a period of time.

It is the embodiment of what Jesus meant when he said *"What you sow you shall reap"*, or *" Do not do to others what you do not want done to yourself"*. Jesus, the master teacher knew that we are one, and if you are awakened you realize that what you do unto another you truly do unto yourself. An awakened human being clears as he creates, and flows like the river towards the sea. As he creates, he is conscious of the consequences in the moment he is creating, so that it can be transformed or erased.

When you awaken there is no heaviness in the way you act, thus there is no bad karma. There is a lightness and grace around conscious people, who appear to be easy going and lucky. Luck is only the reading of the universal library of signs, where all good things come your way when you act according to your most intimate nature, which is love. Conscious people seem like they float through life, and dance to the rhythm of the song they choose.

To clear the karma is to be conscious of the effect that your action is going to cause, and to decide not to do something because of the negative effect or lack of higher good for all included.

To eradicate karma you need to be conscious of what you do, be conscious of your actions. You transform your karma by being in your heart and consciously acting for the greater good of all involved and in that way stopping new karma from being created. In the twin soul union twin souls help each other resolve karmic issues with other people. Even if there are some karmic events from 'past lives' between twins they come from a higher awareness and can deal with them easily, their love will be the guiding light towards resolving and forgiving any hurts they previously experienced.

Lapse of duality

We are expanding always even if we are not aware of it consciously, every second we expand because in every next second we are not the same.

Expansion is beautiful and ever flowing, and the beauty of us as human beings is that we are always evolving, growing and becoming more. Through the twin soul journey we are never alone and abandoned and one of the biggest illusions on this planet is that we are separate from creation and God/Goddess.
In future years the science is going to catch up on our inner knowing and 'prove' beyond a doubt that this is true. When we awaken, we see the duality for what it is, we do not identify with it because we are no longer in the game of identification with anything.

To identify with the lie of the world is to live in the Matrix, to live in the Illusion.

We embraced our Divinity, we know who we are and are just observers of the experience we have. We are so cared for and loved with all of the celestial helpers at our disposal helping us with our evolution; we just have to see it. Everything is serving us and that is a wonderful knowing.

Meditation
Forgiving your ancestors through unconditional love

The purpose of this meditation is clearing your ancestors lineage of all that is not of the highest good for your Union and soul integration.

All of your ancestors are built up into a single point of expression which is you. To go forward in creating new worlds we must acknowledge this and give forgiveness and love to all of our ancestors, for all that was manifested through them. Even if this manifesting was done through fear and ignorance we must give forgiveness to all who walked the earth before us.

Twin souls usually incarnate into very dysfunctional families who have lots of negative patterning that influences them. This meditation will bring awareness that you are doing everything together with your twin even if most of the time the ego has you believe that you are alone. Know that you are not alone.

Find a peaceful and calm space where nobody will interrupt you for a while. Lie down or sit, whichever feels more comfortable for you. Close your eyes and take a few deep breaths.

In your inner vision see your twin sitting beside you or invite their essence energy to come forth into your presence if you have not met them physically. Sit with them in a beautiful setting of your choice, a beach, a forest, a beautiful waterfall. Or a place where you used to meet, wherever it feels nice for you, wherever you feel safe and loved.

Now hug your twin and while you hug each other feel that pureness of Divine love. Embrace each other in this warm loving energy. Feel your joined hearts beating and the radiating power of your joined energy field.

As you hug each other envision all your radiating chakras merge together in harmony. They fuse so harmoniously and create a beautiful bright light. And now envision that from your joined hearts a fuchsia coloured balloon is exiting to form a third energy of purest love and is ready to enwrap everybody who needs it.

First of all, envision all of your ancestors standing in front of you up to and including your parents' generation.

Your great grandparents, grandparents, your parents, see them standing in front of you.

You do not have to know what they looked like.

This envisioning need only be in the form of energy.

The important thing is that energy is acknowledged, and cleared. Wrap them all into this beautiful fuchsia coloured balloon and say aloud ;*'I forgive all the ignorance, all the fear, and all the pain caused by my ancestors that is still evident in my life through my genetic lineage and I cleanse all of this with unconditional love'.*

As you say this, feel this heavy energy in the form of smoke lift out of them to be absorbed into the light. Now see them all enjoying themselves, smiling and happy. Now turn your back to them and imagine your mother and father giving you a gentle push on the back and blessing you.

Say this to yourself; *'My destiny is my own creation and has nothing to do with my parents and my lineage. I am free to go wherever my heart leads me without the baggage of my family and my ancestors'.*

Imagine your heart love is pouring into all for the healing and recognition of their hearts. You are standing in front of all these people and giving this compassionate, unconditional love energy. See all of these lineages cleared now and be thankful for all of the teachings.

You are closing these karmic patterns from your family templates and you are changing and cleansing them through your twin soul love. Now see this pink light embracing all of them and feel the relief. Now turn to your twin look at them and say to them; *'I love you unconditionally and we know this love is alive and true. Your happiness is my happiness'.* Tell them in your heart that no matter what, you are with them helping along the way and every step of the way. This is to release your twin from any kind of expectation regarding anything relating to your Union, so you can easily let the love flow between the two of you.

This soul love is so innocent and pure; it is the return to innocence itself when love was a state of being rather than a state of doing. Be with them and feel your heart opening with each beat.

When you are ready, open your eyes.

You are blessed, for being able to feel this oneness and this beauty. Know this and own this feeling.

Come back to this love every time you need it.

Invocation
Coming home

My light, heart of my heart
we came here to remember.
To spread this light from our hearts into the world
this is our gift to all, to beauty, to peace, to joy.
This love is a gift to each other.
This world is our field of play and joy.
Remember.
I am calling you, listen.
Your heart is whispering come home, come home.
Come home to me my Beloved,
where your only home is.
You know that place of peace and stillness,
my Beloved, my one and only.
It is time, it is time.

CHAPTER FOURTEEN

SIGNING UP FOR THE ASCENSION OF PLANET EARTH

' Age has no reality except in the physical world. The essence of a human being is resistant to the passage of time. Our inner lives are eternal which is to say that our spirits remain as youthful and vigorous as when we were in full bloom. Think of love as a state of grace, not the means to anything, but the alpha and omega, an end in itself '.

Gabriel Garcia Marquez, Love in the time of cholera

*"Do not wait for leaders.
Do it alone; person to person".*

Mother Teresa

Awakening into the body

As we make contracts on earth for so many things, so we make contracts on the higher planes of existence as well. We stand side by side with our ascended master teachers, and choose what we want to experience and solve in each lifetime.

You signed up and volunteered for the planet Earth at this time in history. None of us is here on Earth by accident. The age of Pisces has ended, and the Age of Aquarius is in front of us with all its changes.

We as a species are ascending and everything is quickening, but at the same time, we can feel and see that external sources are trying to keep us in fear. We have all this technology which enables us to connect globally and use it for the benefit of all the people on the planet.

If you are aware, you can see that what used to be one year of time does not appear so anymore. Now one year seems more like six months in terms of experiencing and learning and it is going to quicken even more as we collectively rise in consciousness. Our soul contracts can last as long as we need and we have already sealed these contracts before we incarnate here on Earth.

As soul beings, which in essence we are, we can simultaneously exist in multidimensional realities because the soul is non-local and can perceive many experiences at the same time, even if our conscious mind is not aware of these realities. The mind is adjusted this way in order not to be burdened with remembering too much information, because our body is of this earth, but our soul is universal.

This is why there is no death, we only change the coat that we call our body. Our memory and our consciousness is adapted for this time/ space reality on earth, meaning that we came here with a certain amnesia.

The awakening process which is occurring for so many people on the planet at this time is the remembering process of who we truly are.

We are remembering that we are not here by accident, that we are not 'dropped' here on earth without a purpose.

You can have very many different outfits but the one who wears them is the same.

[handwritten: THE LIGHT? which happens when sperm enters the egg.]

When we die, we only enter a different dimensional reality. Before we were born we did not know this world existed and it seemed that at the minute we were born we died to the old world, this world we knew was our mother's womb, our home for nine months. The same way we 'die' here on earth just to be born into another world. We are curious beings and we wished to come here to earth to have a bodily experience, and sometimes we get lost in all of the sensations the body has to offer. When we enter this spiritual game, we sometimes don't appreciate the major role played by the body.

The body is so important because it is the temple of our soul during our time spent on earth. I think it is very important to learn how to be spiritual in the body. We are still learning how to fully integrate, and this means integrating the mind, the body, and the spirit. We were trying to deny the body for so long, pretending that all that comes from the body is not spiritual. This strong programming came from the organized religions who put the stigma of shame on the body. This is an old paradigm now because we know that without this body we would not be able to do so many wonderful things, like smell, touch, feel, and see with our eyes, experience pleasure.

We can do all of this with our energy, but the body and the senses have their own unique beauty. We should cherish the body we chose to have for this experience. During the process of ascension, it is very important not to pollute your body with toxins, heavy processed food, alcohol, or drugs.

Your body is going to 'ask' you to fast and cleanse itself as you ascend and become lighter. The cleaner the body, the faster you are going to awaken. Our body is a vehicle we borrowed and we use it as long as we are on earth and then we go to other places of existence where we get another body, but one much lighter and higher in vibration. The higher the vibration the less dense the body appears, ethereal and transparent, like a cloak of energy. It appears as if light, and of light it is, while here on earth it appears solid. But in reality we are all made of light.

Knowing who we are

By this time on a twin soul journey, you begin to live and breathe love and that becomes your only concern. You live your new way of life and are the leader instead of waiting for somebody else to show you the way. We accumulated all of this knowledge through all these lives not to keep it for ourselves but to share it, and share it through action.

A true integrated soul will go forward and share the gifts they have with everybody. Because you are ripe, you cannot contain your knowing and beauty within you anymore. Your inner knowing has to flow, for the benefit of all.

The God/Goddess of truth and love is in you and you know it. This unconditional love vibrates out of your energy field and people and circumstances are drawn to you. Our planet Earth is ascending in unison with us for the more peaceful and beautiful reality which we are creating.

The collective mission of twin soul love is for all the twin souls around the planet to create many sparks, so they can ignite the fire of love into the collective, and transform this planet into a higher vibration reality.

Therefore, it is possible to achieve this peaceful life on earth. Each one of us has a responsibility to contribute in our own way to the collective. A human being cannot be greedy and selfish anymore and only satisfy his survival needs; an awakened human being does not live on survival mode any longer. He is in harmony with his heart, with nature and the whole of existence and wants to benefit the whole.

Living and breathing love

All of us humans in reality are one Source love, and what we do individually reflects through the whole.

Once your soul has been ignited you are never the same again. The ignition of the sacred heart can do miracles.

Believe this. Know this. Own this. In my heart I cherish the vision of these ignited beautiful hearts full of this sacred love going forth and living in truth and peace, this is the truth and needs only to become visible for all of us to experience it in this three dimensional reality. From my perspective, living the love means having compassion for the people we live with, having compassion for the world of suffering, forgiving more, smiling more, giving a helping hand to those who are in need and most important of all empowering people to see their own divinity.

The most important help we can give as twin souls and healers is to show people the way how to heal and love themselves and become more conscious.

Then we can share the riches of this planet evenly, so that everybody can enjoy their experience on Earth. Everybody who is born into this planet deserves to live their life in peace, and raise their children in health and happiness. If we love our hearts, that love will flow onto others, though I acknowledge in my deepest heart that there are no others, we are all one consciousness, so when we love ourselves we love the whole world at the same time.

The God/Goddess truth

What does the word 'God' mean? I don't like to use the word God as a metaphor for the long bearded punishing man up in the sky, and I do not use this word as a description of some outside force that is separate from myself. I refer to the word 'God' in order to depict the Divine, the Source, Higher Intelligence, or whatever you like to call this energy of presence. This energy for me is not masculine, but both masculine and feminine. This is why I use the God/Goddess expression. The punishing entity in the sky is not my representation of God. I like to think of God as the Presence. I like to think of God as the feeling of love and peace.

My experience has taught me that if love and peace are present God must be near. God is love. Love is God.

If I am in the presence of a person, whom I feel energetically is emanating love and peace, I am not interested in what they believe, or if they go to a church or a synagogue.

Remember you can mask yourself with all kinds of religious beliefs but energy never lies.

A person who is healed and one with God/Goddess, has a certain aura of love, a certain vibration and you cannot fake that. Love never lies. Either love is present in a person or not. I would rather say 'awakened', because love always lies dormant there inside of us, buried underneath our own conditioning. A belief in God in organized religions is often an excuse for people to behave as they like, meaning that they have all these rules and rules get distorted by the ones who use them. Organized religions act as if they know God, and for me that in itself is arrogance.

God cannot be known, it can only be experienced as a mystery. God is, and there is nowhere that God is not, omnipresent, omnipotent. You as a human being are in the heart of the creation, nourished and loved, taken care of, provided with all the abundance.

I love this saying; *"Love is not coming into something that you don't intimately know, but rather shedding everything that was in the way of that recognition"*. We must stand in that recognition that we are made of love, made for love.

Meditation
Blessing the earth with happy healed humans

The purpose of this meditation is to send healing energy and heal the Earth with our own happiness.

As we know, we can only give what we already have. We can nourish our planet by being conscious about the suffering we cause to ourselves, to others and to Mother Earth. This meditation is about healing together with our Mother Earth.

This meditation serves to bring to attention that our intention is at the centre of creation. We came here to create, and everything we created, every object or thing, was imagined before it was expressed in reality.

Find a calm and peaceful place where you can be with yourself for a while. Lie or sit down, whatever you prefer. Close your eyes and breathe deeply a few times so you can relax.

Now in your inner vision you are going to travel around the planet and recognize its beauty and see all the humans of the planet healed and happy.

Firstly, you go to Africa, the beautiful cradle of humanity and look at all the children fed and happy, smiling. There is no hunger anymore, no greed, or limited resources. See clearly how there is enough abundance for everyone, wherever there is war see it end, and people hug each other and forgive.

See loving people helping each other and living in peace. Now, go to Europe and see a peaceful, abundant, just continent and its people flourishing, eating healthy foods, caring for each other, protecting the weaker. See rich soil abundant with fresh organic food, with enough food for everyone. Now let us go to Asia and see these beautiful people free, wherever there is oppression see freedom, see the freedom of speech. People can express their opinions freely.

Let us go to Australia and see all of the beautiful nature, people are free to express themselves and ready to spread the message of love. Now go to North and South America and see the poverty gone, there is equality between people, no more racism but honouring the differences, people are sharing their goods and there are enough resources for everybody. You see people content and celebrating their humanity. Now see Antarctica and the beauty of the eternal ice in balance to sustain our planet's ecosystem. The planet is breathing as one, see it, and feel it. It is possible.

Say this out aloud; *'The new reality of this healed planet is here, and so it is. Amen'*. When you want to leave this creation, open your eyes and know that you created a new earth with your intention. Relax and breathe deeply and with every breath you feel the life force in you. You relax more and more.

Now see in front of you a small version of planet Earth with all life currently present on it and say out loud; *'With my unconditional sacred heart I bless all life you hold oh Beloved mother. I bless all the suffering, all the joy, all the heartbeats, and all the visible and invisible life. From my wide heart let love go to your heart. Thank you, thank you'*.

Now hold your hands above the planet and see the light coming from your heart going into your hands and bathing the planet. You feel the force of your love and you know in this moment that you are a creator of everything beautiful. Feel the joy of your contribution of love and stay in this peace. Now imagine the seven billion people who are on the planet currently doing the same, such is the power of our love. Bless yourself in the end. May I be blessed, may I be blessed.

Invocation
Fountain of love

*This love is burning through eternity
connecting us through the heart,
so we can know peace, joy and self love.
As we embrace ourselves completely
 we clearly see what this love has done.
It has opened our hearts like two lotus
flowers so fragrant and beautiful.
We are so vulnerable my love and that is the place
where love touches us in grace and beauty.
We dive into this love with each breath
and let anybody who needs drink from this fountain.
Thank you, I love you.
Thank you, I love you.*

CHAPTER FIFTEEN

HEALING THE EARTH

" Important encounters are planned by the souls long before the bodies see each other ".

Paulo Coelho

*"We do not inherit the earth from our ancestors
We borrow it from our children".*

Native American saying

Giving the love vibrations to Earth

*A*s we collectively evolve and know that we are one with our planet earth we give and take from her in a more conscious way. Into earth we go once we die, into ashes we turn and we become one again.
As we raise our vibrations into the higher frequency, we raise the vibration of the earth as well. We are her children and she is our beautiful mother. The child can sometimes take advantage of a mother's love and not perceive how much she constantly gives, and our mother earth gives to us all the time. She would never not give us food or shelter, but at this moment in time, I feel she is tired.
Her energy needs new recourses and inputs. We have to look through our spiritual eyes and stop what we have been doing while we still have time to bring the balance back to this planet.
 At first we do this one by one, as individuals.

We have to honour the place we call home, we just borrowed this place to live for a short span of time and we are obligated to leave it to our children.

We borrowed this planet from our children, as the Native American saying states, and if you have to give back that which you borrowed, in what state would you return it to your children and grandchildren? Every human who is currently living on this planet and claims that he loves his children, must ask himself if that is so, why does he continue to destroy this planet? We must be aware of the impact that one individual has on this planet, from the smallest things like leaving the water running while you brush your teeth, to throwing away food, to buying things you don't need. From blind consumerism of every kind, all the way to the bigger challenges we are facing today like pollution of the oceans and the air.

We must become conscious that 'small' things become big through the accumulative effect. Every action in this universe has its reaction, even the smallest one. Only an unconscious person thinks that an individual has no impact on the overall existence.

We are individuals but at the same time, we are a mass of consciousness and we affect each other all of the time. Now is the time that we are ending all contracts that are harmful for us so that we can leap into this new life on earth, the five dimensional earth reality where life will be more harmonious for all of us. This present three dimensional reality will not disappear and the world will not change overnight but as we change, eventually it will transform and become a different place in which to live. The result of our changed beliefs and behaviours will be a changed world.

In the fifth dimensional reality where we will live from our hearts, we will know that it is time for us to start changing and start creating this heaven on earth, and make choices consciously for the benefit of all. Who is going to do it? We are going to do it, all together. We are going to do it one by one.

Closing the karmic soul contracts

Closing soul contracts is very important for our collective ascension. What does it mean to close the soul contract? This means to be so in tune with your real self that you know and feel intuitively when a certain soul mate relationship has finished, and you are acutely aware of what you have learned from it.

It means that you so love yourself that you clearly see everything that a certain relationship has taught you, and when you feel that there is no more expansion in that relationship, you consciously decide to let that person go. I don't refer only to romantic relationships here but to any soul mate relationship in your life. You let them go in the most beautiful and gentle way for the benefit of all involved.

You wish upon them the greatest journey they can have for the expansion of their soul.

There is a big difference between ending a relationship consciously, or unconsciously as a route for escape. If you end a relationship from the space of peace and love, everyone involved benefits.

The love you have for a certain soul mate or a soul mate partner can never be lost, but first you must understand that love is not ownership. Love is free. Love is what you are, it is the state of being that you are in. In today's society, we still may feel forced by cultural expectations or religious influences to remain in marital relationships 'till death do us apart'. This is such an ancient paradigm and we can clearly see that in its traditional manifestation, it does not work any longer. We all evolve and change with the passing of time and it is perhaps unrealistic to expect that two people who met in their twenties would have the same desires, outlooks and goals in their fifties, and this is completely acceptable. We have to evolve from this fervent indoctrination of organized religions on the concepts of relationships and marriages.

They always state that the traditional family unit is the foundation stone of society, but in my opinion, this is not strictly true. I say that there are many versions of 'family' and only the healthy, nourishing and conscious relationships are the foundation stone of the future society.

What price are we paying if we stay in these 'obligatory' marital contracts out of security, co-dependence, safety, and conformity? I am not saying that people should just get divorced and not persevere and endure setbacks but rather that they should know when they have outgrown a certain relationship and when it is time to end it.

I am advocating for healthy, unconditional, evolved relationships. Many of the ills of society today are just a reflection of these miserable marriages or settlements. Pre-arranged marriages, which are still present in many cultures on our planet, is a subject worthy of its own discussion, but suffice it to say that too many people have suffered and lost their lives from these contracts.

You are probably now asking yourself if the freedom to have relationships without any marriage contract would result in a society that is utterly promiscuous and without any moral constraints.

Well, I don't believe so because a conscious person is in tune with themselves and has a self-regulatory mechanism which creates as much harmony within as without. Today we have this maladjusted society full of insane rules, and I am saying that a conscious person can relate in a completely different way. A conscious person does not need restrictions and is aware that everything he does must bring the highest good for everyone involved.

We need to start to reinvent relating with each other. To end a relationship unconsciously means to create more karma and push the repeat button until you learn the lesson.

This is why people keep repeating the same patterns of behaviour and relationships because they look outside for the reasons why something does not work. The reason is hidden deep inside of you, and I know that sometimes in the short run it is easier to turn away than to look inside. You are balancing all of the karma and are now in a state of wishing the greatest harmony for yourself inside and out. The person who is with you at the time will bless your journey if he/she is conscious and if not you still have to do your own thing. We must know that we came here alone and no two souls evolve at the same pace. This is why these discords happen when it feels that one partner has 'gone further' and the other one feels 'left behind'.

Your twin soul, as the ultimate mirror, will justly reflect that which you represent and what you are. That is why you cannot be with your twin before Divine timing. This connection is Divine, as is this journey and you wouldn't endure the strength of this connection if you experienced it before you were ready.

For everything there is a season in this universe and it is all divinely orchestrated. I can already smell the fragrance of the new earth which we are approaching. One by one into this love revolution. Changing our hearts and loving ourselves so much that we see ourselves in the other. That is the true meaning of brotherhood and sisterhood. We can have this heaven on earth if we wish to, and we are wishing it collectively now. When this new reality is going to fully manifest depends on all of us.

The more of us who wish the same, the more the outer reality will change according to our collective wish and that is why it is so important for each one of us to work on ourselves.

We will start living for each other instead of against each other. We will start to cooperate instead of compete. We will start to create a new society based on talent, nurturing the inner way and enhancing each other's abilities. We will know no more borders, nationalities and races, because in our hearts we will experience the oneness. We are nothing more than one human race. We are human beings. Feel that word, human. We will enhance our beauty through our differences and not be divided because of them. The differences will bring us together and bring richness to our own experience.

Our hearts will be open completely so that we can telepathically communicate through the heart consciousness. We are paving the way for generations to come and we have a big responsibility to leave this place better than it was when we came here.

Each one of us should ask ourselves; 'did I leave this place better, did I do my best? Is my heart at peace?' When we can honestly answer 'yes' to all of these questions the planet will know peace and we will become an evolved race that we call human. One heart, one humanity, this is my dream. Let us dream it together.

The fragrance of new Earth

The fragrance of this new earth can be inhaled already by sensitive empaths and conscious beings. The vision of this new earth is seen first inside of the heart where all manifestation comes from and then on the outside. To have faith and believe is to firstly see the seed of your own pure potential, that potential is waiting for you to water and nourish it in its desire to become whatever it wants.

We see the potential of this new possibility; we see the love coming through the veils of illusion. Don't fool yourself with the current three dimensional reality and how the world looks at the moment, don't get stuck on what the media is telling you, while keeping you in fear. Fear is here and love is here as well.

The question is what will you choose? You know this kingdom inside of you intimately, it feels like it has been waiting patiently for a long time to break through.

In this vision we see this truth and as twin souls we are on the threshold of the leading edge of this new earth manifestation. It is we who are making this change constantly, bit by bit, systematically, day in and day out. Let us embrace our creation and become conscious of what we are creating in each moment, and then take action. The un-manifested is waiting for us in the fields of imagination, so we can tap into it and create.

The imagination is the evidence of the divine.

The imagination is the field of many potential timelines from which we can choose to manifest. We have it for a reason, so how are we using this divine tool? Pure potential is always pulsating around us; the question is what do we all want to create together? What are we imagining this world into becoming?

Living truly for each other

Living for each other means seeing truly who we are and then connecting on that basis with others. In my opinion there are no others, we are but one living organism in the dream of creation. We have to see clearly through the paradox of creation, meaning that we are not much more important than an ant, and at the same time, we are more important than a star. We are standing in the middle of absurdity.

The highest truth and the most absurd are one and the same and we can never understand this with our limited mind.

We don't have to understand everything with our ego mind, we just have to be and the knowing is there. Be present and share what comes through you, nothing else. We do not own the knowledge, the knowledge just comes through us; everything comes through us to share with others.

Nothing is ours, nothing. Each piece of art, literature, music that is created just came through, for the benefit of all. We do not create anything, life creates through us if we allow it.

It just comes through us and is dispersed into the wider world. Why would we want to hold on to the knowledge merely for our own benefit? We cannot hold the wind, the river, and the rays of sun upon our skin but we feel them and share that joy with others around us. We are nothing and everything all at the same time, grasp that, and you come to a place of grace and mercy. When we open the door of our compassion, the love floods our life and we bathe in it, and naturally, we touch everybody whom we encounter in our daily lives. You come to a place of mystery and wonder. That is why I do not favour organized religions because they act as though they have the answers for our human existence. I think they do not. Nevertheless, you have to be humble to admit that you do not know.

The true religious heart for me is the mysterious heart. Life is a beautiful mystery and we do not know all the answers. That is true humility and religion.

We can hide many things but love cannot stay hidden, because her only wish is to be expressed and shared.

Meditation
Healing planet Earth

The purpose of this meditation is healing the Earth and being aware of the input we all have. We have to see this heaven on earth in which we live and it is just a matter of perceiving it so. As we heal ourselves, we heal the earth at the same time. This meditation will show you that your part in creating this new abundant earth is very important and that we were always a part of the Earth's body.

Find a calm space where you won't be disturbed for half an hour, lay down or sit down, as you wish. Close your eyes and breathe, feel your breath of life coming in and out of your body and feel the aliveness in you. See and feel the energy stream through your entire body from head to toes. Relax more with very breath you take.
 Now see in your inner eye the planet standing in front of you. It is our beloved mother earth and our home where we chose to live and create. Now see the planet glowing with energy and radiating the beautiful magenta pink, the colour of love. It is glowing with love, peace, nourishment, fresh food and water, rich soils, and abundance beyond measure. Imagine her giving us all of these gifts and feeling happy.
Breathe with joy through her trees, flowing with her rivers and resting into the waves of the seas. See all of the animals free and loving their young. See clearly that they have their own purpose on earth. Imagine the magnificence and the beauty of the planet where we live, in the mountains, the beaches, and the oceans.

Earth is our home and how you treat your home is how you treat yourself. She is lush and green, colourful, abundant with fresh air, pregnant with life and richness. She is full of energy resources we can use for the elevation of our current condition on the planet. Envision the free solar and wind energy we can use for our benefit. She wants to give and share with us all of the abundance she possesses.

From your heart, there is a stream of light bathing her, and you can see her glowing more and more until she is one ball of light. Feel this beauty and know that there is more than enough for all of us. You call all the Archangels and invite them to come and stay here with you, and help transform the old and give birth to the new. You see them like raindrops entering the earth, so that they can guard this new energy. You see this wave of energy from the galaxy bathing her, and see how every wave makes her more radiant. This is happening right now and so be it.

Say this aloud; *'I see this planet Earth radiant and glowing so full of energy and love, in peace and abundance '. Amen.* When you have had enough time, relax and breathe, and stay a bit in silence. Know in your being that the Earth is healed and happy.

Invocation
One love

We are light and love, nothing
but light and love, made for love, made out of love.
We are brothers and sisters, all the same,
we know this truth and are remembering now.
So we can all return to innocence,
so we all return home.
We are one.
One humanity held in the palm of the Divine.
One love for one heartbeat.
One dream out of the Divine dream.
One Source of Love.
We are one.

QUESTIONS AND ANSWERS:

1. What is a twin flame/twin soul?
It is your Divine expression, your soul spark expressing itself through two bodies. You and your twin are one soul experiencing life through two bodies.

2. Do we have only one twin soul?
We have only one twin soul for the experience of union of masculine and feminine in the Divine embrace.

3. What is the difference between the soul mate and the twin soul?
The difference is that a soul mate is another soul from your soul family or from a different soul family helping you on your journey, and a twin soul is you, your own soul divided for the learning of the same knowledge from two different perspectives.

4. What are the signs of meeting your twin soul?
Soul recognition, love at first sight, an unusual meeting, separation, telepathic connection, spiritual awakening, mission, soul attraction, strong synchronicities, dream visions, shared 'past lives', a feeling of completion.

5. Does everybody have a twin soul?
I believe everybody in essence is a twin soul but not all of us wished to incarnate with our twin at this time, but even if you chose not to be embodied together, your twin soul is always with you in spirit and can guide you here on Earth.

6. How long can a twin soul journey last?
This journey is eternal and does not bend to linear time as we know it, it goes on through many life times. But in the linear time we

have here on earth, it can last from five, ten, twenty, thirty years, as each twin soul journey is unique and different. A mutual characteristic for all who are on this journey is that it is a process and for such a soul journey, you need time.

7. How do I know when I have found my twin soul?
You might not know it consciously in the moment of meeting your twin but you will know in the moment as of awakening from a dream and you will see that your whole life has been preparing you for this experience. When you wake up you will see that every little thing in your life lead you to the revelation of this truth. You will know it.

8. Can I choose to find a twin soul?
You can consciously choose by doing the inner work to find a Divine partner to create a higher vibrational soul mate relationship, but you cannot choose a twin soul that way. Together with your twin you chose this journey before incarnation. We can say that the twin soul journey finds you. Everything is planned prior to incarnation. You are on this path even if you are not aware of it. It reveals its secrets to you when the time is right, and then you know. This is not an easy journey and if you are on this path, you will know it.

9. Can twin souls be the same gender?
Yes, they can be the same gender because the soul does not have a gender, and it cares only for expressing itself through the masculine and feminine energy and the energy can express through any body, male or female. The energy of our soul is neither masculine nor feminine.

10. Am I betraying my twin if I am with other soul mates?
No, you are not betraying them. You and your twin are connected always and this bond is unbreakable by anybody. The experiences

with soul mates are essential for your human expansion, they are essential for your growth until you have arrived at the maturity to come into union.

11. What is the age difference between twin souls?
This can vary, from a few years to bigger age differences and there are no set rules because each twin journey is unique, but since this journey has so many obstacles to overcome, including incarnating in different races, nationalities, countries, or dysfunctional families, one of the obstacles can present itself as a large age difference. It all depends on what both twins chose to overcome.

12. Can twin souls be married to others, or have children with soul mates when they meet?
Yes, and they usually do. The harder the circumstances the harder they have to work to overcome them for the Union. Do you think that God would make it easy for you to know true love? Well, this connection doesn't function as soul mate relationships do. Remember that this is not a regular relationship; this is firstly a spiritual Divine connection, a Union between two people.

13. Why is this experience so hard and painful?
It is painful because its purpose is to help you expand and come into Christ's consciousness. You chose this experience firstly to achieve your highest potential, and secondly to become the embodied love, and this is not easy to do.

14. Do twin souls have a mission together?
They certainly do. They chose this experience firstly to become their incarnated higher selves in expression and to come into union with God/Goddess. Secondly, to anchor this unconditional love they feel for each other into the body, and thirdly, to lead everybody into a new way of relating and being on this new earth, by their example. A couple who endures this journey and comes

into union vibrates at a very high vibration of unconditional love. This love affects everything.

15. Can one twin still do the mission alone before the union happens?

Yes, one twin can do the mission although it does not reach the fullest potential of how it would be when they enter the Union. The primary goal of this connection is for each of them to become the best version of themselves first and then to create even more miracles together. When they enter the Union and come together in the physical form the mission is on full force potential.

16. Sometimes this path is so hard that I think of giving up on this connection.

I know it is the most challenging experience but you cannot give up on your twin because it is the same as if you have given up on yourself. When you are unconscious in life it is easy to lie to yourself, but once awakened you have to go on because the betrayal of self, hurts too much. So do the inner work, pray, visualize, trust and have patience in Divine timing.

17. I feel so misunderstood in this journey, what should I do?

The twin soul path is a lonely journey because no one from the three dimensional perspective of reality can understand what you are going through, and often friends and family judge you. Do not ask for reassurance from friends and family because they don't understand what you are going through. You have to start to communicate with your soul family, spiritual guides, angels, archangels to get help. Nourish your connection to Source always. No man can give you the comfort you seek. It is your journey to the Divine, your most intimate journey. You have all the answers inside of you. Trust yourself.

18. Sometimes I have so many doubts, does this mean that this person is not my twin soul?
This is normal because we are still human and it does not mean that this person is not your twin; If it is your true twin you will know and feel that your twin is slowly leading you to God/Goddess and unconditional love. On this journey your ego is going to test and torture you in unimaginable ways, but when in doubt just remember how far you have already come, and remember that God/Goddess doesn't give a promise that cannot be kept. This promise lies within you and it is going to be fulfilled and completed.

19. Do I have to be in contact with my twin for this journey to unfold?
No, this is not a rule. This process of coming into union is firstly internal and your twin is always with you even if you are not physically together or in communication. You must understand that you are together in fifth dimensional reality always, even if you are not in contact. The separation is the biggest illusion of this connection.

20. When will I be with my twin?
As you come into Union from within you will feel the timeline approaching but you still have to wait for the Divine timing. This Union will not happen a moment before it is time.

21. Why did we choose this experience?
So that we can know the Self, so that we can know the Divine.

22. How is the sexuality different in a twin flame relationship?
It is very much different because since nothing can stay hidden between twin souls, so it is with the intimate sexual expression. They make love in their second bodies, not only with their physical

bodies for the purpose of pleasure and this is very intense. When twin souls connect, they sexually merge with all of their chakras and this can be literally felt in their energies. In other words, twins heal each other in the sexual act and merge all of their bodies together. The sexual act between twin souls makes for the creation of this third energy, which is very powerful and tangible as it is sent into the world in the moment of sexual creation between the two of them. The sexual act between twin souls is truly sacred.

23. Do twin souls look the same physically?

Their similarities do not have to be physical. This is not a physical thing although it sometimes can be. This has more to do with how the energy is coming through them and appearing the same. Then it looks as if this energy overlaps physically when you look at them together. This same energy, soul frequency, comes from the inside, as with siblings for example, you see that they are different but at the same time you can see that they come from the same parents. It is similar with twin souls; you can see that they come from one soul. All twin pairs have the exact same soul frequency. It is a frequency thing and people who are more psychic and empathic can feel this. You can sometimes notice how they have the same expression when they smile, or the way they make a move, or the way they hold their body, they can have similar features, like the eyes. So many times I have experienced my twin laughing through me. My point is that this is very subtle but everyone will feel and see that they are as one. When they stand together side by side people will feel how powerful they are. You know how birth twins are very similar, but each have their own characteristics, it's somewhat like that.

24. Why do I feel so alone in this twin soul mission?

Because every warrior of the heart has to go through being alone, he cannot face himself if the crowd is always behind him. The solitude is essential for shaping your inner vision related to this mission. When you are ready, you will integrate and eventually come back. You can feel alone even if you are among people, and you can connect with people who are experiencing the same, but in the end one must face this journey alone first. When you connect to the Source, Divine helpers, Ascended masters, Archangels, angels, spiritual guides it becomes a bit easier, because they can assist you with so many things during the process of healing, but ultimately it is your journey.

25. Who knows first about the connection, the male or the female?
There are no set rules but usually it is the female who understands first because the female is more connected with her emotional body and feelings, though as I said, the male can be very conscious of the connection too but expresses it differently.

26. How can I come to Union faster?
There is nothing you can do from the 'outside' that will bring you into union with your twin soul faster. It is an internal process. You have to be willing to do the inner work, to walk the talk; you have to be willing to look deeply into yourself and heal and integrate all aspects of you that are unconscious, the aspects of you that that you reject. Embrace the shadow self. As you heal you come more into the frequency of unconditional love, and that will attract your twin back into your life and the union will happen, providing both do the work.

27. I heard there are a few waves of twins, is that true?
Through my understanding and experience of twin souls, I have noticed that you can classify them into three waves. People who are on this twin soul path born from 1940-1960 would be the first wave and these are the people now in their middle fifties to late seventies. The second wave would be twins born from 1970-1990 who are now in their thirties to late forties, and the third wave

would be twins born from 1990 onwards and these are twins in their twenties now. Each wave has a specific task in this twin soul collective mission. You must understand that these are the approximate values as they were transmitted to me, and that variations can occur.

28. When do I recognize that I am on a twin soul journey?
You recognize this journey unconsciously in childhood. In my own experience I always felt like I had somebody the same as me walking somewhere on this earth like a twin that I was missing, but of course I couldn't express it consciously. As for the conscious recognition, you will wake up some more when you meet your twin in the flesh, and then as the journey continues at the chosen time of your soul awakening you will know for sure.

29. What does it mean to do the inner work?
Doing the inner work means looking at yourself and all that appears as shadow and dark in you with all of your honesty and love. You can pray, meditate, spend time in silence, do inner child work, work with sound, do affirmation work. Today we have so many techniques to choose from so that we can bring healing into our lives. But, I want to accentuate that all of the techniques are just road maps and you should not get stuck in any technique. Experiment with all of them until you find your own truth. The rejection of self needs to be embraced and exposed to the light of consciousness. It literally means travelling through time with your consciousness so that you can integrate all aspects of yourself. In the end it means loving yourself completely as you are, and if you want to take it further you transcend this 'self' and through love for yourself you find love for all existence.

30. How can I know that I am on the right path?
There is no right or wrong path in the now, the eternal now. If you are going through a certain experience, you are on your right path

for your highest evolution in that particular moment. Ask yourself who is judging the present moment and looking for another experience instead of the experience that is presented to you? All ways lead to your completion and your highest good or otherwise you would not be where you are.

31. Why do I feel such pain when 'separated' from my twin?

All of this pain you feel is the pain of rejecting your soul recognition, it is rejection of the true self and that always hurts. That is why the separation in the physical occurs in the first place, because both twins are in resistance of their true Divine nature, in other words they are staying in their false self identities until they awake to the truth of this connection.

32. Can twin souls live in different states?

Yes they can, but it is not so with all twins. All twins have their own obstacles to overcome. Today more than ever, it is easier to connect through technology and many twins can help each other in that way. In my experience when the time comes to meet your twin in the physical realm, everything conspires for you to meet. Vast synchronicities are at play here and even if they live in different countries, they will meet somehow. Nothing is impossible for the Divine intelligence to orchestrate a meeting between two people who are supposed to meet.

33. I feel this weight on my shoulders from doing energy work on behalf of my parents.

What you feel is true and can be very exhausting at times. Both twins have incarnated in very difficult family conditions which make the journey harder for clearing the family template. From an early age they will see what the template of their family is, and work through it as they grow up. Sometimes you are going to have a feeling that you are the adult in the dynamic between you and your parents. As you work on yourself, you are showing them that there is another way of living. You are setting the stage for the new, setting a new template of relating.

34. Do twins have parallel experiences in the physical?

Often they do. They will have the same affinities for foreign countries, languages, and music. Whatever your twin is attracted to, you will be interested in, and vice versa. In my opinion they have the same experience from two different angles, because remember that your twin is you. In the higher dimensional reality, they are working together as one, on all of their tasks. Here in this reality they are one soul in two bodies. In my understanding, they can have opposite sides of the same experiences so that they can get two perspectives from one experience. For example, one twin will wish to see how it is to have children early in life and the second twin can choose to do this later, but both will have children. Or one can have many partners and the other can choose to stay with one partner. This way as one soul, they can gain two different perspectives.

35. Can I do my mission without my twin?

You certainly can, but for the benefit of all and the completion of your sacred contract you can amplify your mission when united and working together.

36. Does separation always happen between twin souls?

It does, because the physical separation is needed so that both twins can come into themselves more deeply and this is characteristic of twin soul unions. The separation happens also because they repel each other when they are not conscious of the connection and their inner world. Both twins work the hardest on their individual paths when separated.

37. How can I know if I am in the surrender and illumination phase?

You can know this through the feelings of more peace and calmness, also by the feeling that you do not need to control the outcome of the union anymore. You are at peace with how and when the union is going to happen. You are at peace even if it does not happen in this lifetime. You are at peace. The surrender phase slides into the radiance and illumination, after the surrender the natural thing to do is to shine your light into your life, by starting to undertake your mission. You do whatever you love, and cherish every moment of your life with deep love and gratitude.

38. Do I have to leave my soul mate marriage to be with my twin?

You certainly do not have to do that. It all depends on how you have decided to be together with your twin. Every lasting contract between you and every soul mate must naturally end if you choose so and only if you want it. If you try to force it, or come out of a soul mate contract prematurely, your twin will feel it and know it. They will know that you did not act out of your highest soul alignment and reflect that to you. You made a contract with your spouse too, so if it needs to happen it will in Divine timing.

39. What about the children when you are involved in the experience?

The children are always ok and you must not project from the ego point of view how the children are going to fit into this union. Your children are your twin's spiritual children and vice versa. These children are usually twins themselves. From the Divine perspective of love, children are always protected and cared for. This unconditional love is embedded in their DNA. They are helping your union with their frequency of unconditional love.

40. Why is everybody so obsessed with finding a twin flame?

This is occurring at this time because all of us have this soul remembrance, a feeling that we have somebody who will 'complete us'. We are yearning to connect at a deeper level and in more spiritual ways. Such a soul exists for us even if it's not incarnated on earth at this time. Many people feel the love and guidance from their twin soul in the higher realms of existence. This is so significant at this point in our evolution of consciousness because we are evolving from old ways of relating to each other. Relationships are changing and people feel that they want to connect more deeply with another human being. They want to experience soul love.

41. I feel so alone and incomplete without my twin beside me?

You must know that you are never alone and that the separation is the biggest illusion. Your twin is always with you. When you come into your heart fully you will know and feel this truth. This love that you are searching for is in you and whenever you want, you can tap into its everlasting potential and beauty. Alongside your twin and you, there is your soul family, your guardian angels, your spiritual guides, ascended masters and the Divine. You are never alone. You are already complete.

AFFIRMATIONS
for cultivating and anchoring unconditional love and opening the way into sacred Union.

Affirmations are positive reinforcements that you give to your subconscious mind. The purpose of affirming is reprogramming of your inner negative talk. When you affirm you rewrite your script. What do you want your scenario to sound like? Use these affirmations daily, in the morning before you get up and in the evening before you go to sleep and you will see big changes and improvements in your soul connection and generally in your life.

1. *I AM.*
2. *I AM LOVE.*
3. *I AM LIGHT.*
4. *I AM ALWAYS LOVING, LOVED, AND LOVABLE.*
5. *I DESERVE UNCONDITIONAL LOVE AND I AM ENOUGH.*
6. *I KNOW HOW TO LOVE AND BE LOVED BY MY TWIN SOUL.*
7. *I KNOW HOW TO LOVE MYSELF.*
8. *I LOVE MY INNER CHILD AND I SET HIM/HER FREE.*
9. *IT IS SAFE FOR ME TO EXPRESS WHO I AM.*
10. *IT IS SAFE TO BE ME.*
11. *IT IS SAFE TO LIVE MY TRUTH.*
12. *I EXPRESS THROUGH LOVE.*
13. *I EXPAND THROUGH EXPRESSING LOVE.*
14. *I AM CONNECTED TO MY TWIN SOUL IN UNCONDITIONAL LOVE.*

15. I KNOW HOW TO EXPRESS LOVE TO MY TWIN SOUL.
16. I HEAR AND LISTEN TO MY HIGHER SELF.
17. IT IS SAFE TO EMBODY MY HIGHER SELF.
18. I HAVE A STRONG, HEALTHY BODY.
19. MY BODY CAN RECIEVE HIGHER VIBRATIONS OF LOVE NOW.
20. ALL MY CHAKRAS ARE ALLIGNED AND ROTATING AT THE RIGHT SPEED.
21. I AM CONSTANTLY RECEIVING THE ENERGY FOR THE MANIFESTATION OF MY HIGHEST POTENTIAL.
22. MY TWIN SOUL KNOWS MY LOVE AND I KNOW HIS LOVE.
23. LOVE HAS NO BOUNDARIES AND IT IS UNCONDITIONAL.
24. I KNOW HOW TO BECOME THE BEST VERSION OF MYSELF.
25. I AM THE UNIQUE EXPRESSION OF DIVINE LOVE.
26. I KNOW MY WORTH.
27. I FEEL AND KNOW THE TRUTH OF MY HEART.
28. I KNOW WHAT I KNOW.
29. I AM BEAUTIFUL INSIDE AND OUT.
30. I SEE ALL MY EMOTIONS CLEARLY.
31. I GET CLARITY EVERY DAY.
32. MY TWELVE CHAKRAS ARE ACTIVATING NOW.
33. I AM READY TO RECEIVE ABUNDANCE
34. I AM ABUNDANT.
35. I AM OPEN TO MY INNER GUIDANCE.
36. I LISTEN TO MY HEART.
37. I KNOW WHO I AM.
38. I AM GLOWING INSIDE OUT.
39. I AM A BEAUTIFUL BEING OF DIVINE LOVE.
40. I AM PROTECTED AND CARED FOR.
41. I AM SAFE AND LOVED.
42. I AM IN LOVE WITH LIFE.
43. MY LIFE IS AN EXPRESSION OF THE LOVE I AM.
44. I AM THE QUEEN AND MY TWIN FLAME IS A KING.

45. I AM BALANCED.
46. I AM WHOLE.
47. I AM WITH MY TWIN SOUL ALWAYS.
48. MY TWIN SOUL SEES ME CLEARLY.
49. I SEE MYSELF CLEARLY.
50. I BLESS MY JOURNEY.
51. I SEE MY PURPOSE CLEARLY.
52. I DO WHAT I LOVE.
53. I FEEL JOY WHEN I DO WHAT I LOVE.
54. I KNOW HOW TO FEEL LOVED BY LIFE.
55. I KNOW HOW TO LOVE.
56. I VIBRATE IN THE VIBRATION OF UNCONDITIONAL LOVE.
57. I RADIATE LIGHT.
58. I AM STRONG.
59. I ACCEPT AND LOVE MYSELF COMPLETELY.
60. I LOVE MYSELF, I LOVE MY TWIN SOUL.
61. I AM WORTHY OF ALL THE GOOD IN MY LIFE.
62. I AM GRATEFUL FOR ALL IN MY LIFE.
63. I AM IN UNION WITHIN MYSELF.
64. I AM MANIFESTING MY HIGHEST POTENTIAL.
65. I LOVE LIFE.
66. I LIVE LIFE WITH THE WHOLE OF MY HEART.
67. I HEAR THE WHISPERS OF MY SOUL.
68. I TELEPATHICALLY COMMUNICATE WITH MY TWIN, AND RECEIVE AND GIVE INFORMATION ALL THE TIME.
69. THE DIVINE IS HELPING ME EVERY DAY.
70. I AM GUIDED THROUGH THIS JOURNEY, AND MY SPIRITUAL GUIDES WORK WITH ME FOR MY HIGHEST GOOD.
71. I EMBRACE MY TWIN FLAME JOURNEY COMPLETELY.
72. I GIVE AND RECEIVE UNCONDITIONAL LOVE TO AND FROM MY TWIN SOUL.

73. MY MISSION IS TO LIVE LOVE IN EVERY ASPECT OF MY LIFE.
74. I AM ALIGNED WITH MY HIGHER SELF.
75. I AM ON THE RIGHT PATH, MY PATH.
76. I HAVE COMPASSION FOR MYSELF, AND OTHERS.
77. I TRUST MYSELF.
78. I LOVE BEING ME.
79. I LOVE EXPRESSING THROUGH BEING MYSELF.
80. I AM ON THE DIVINE MISSION WITH MY TWIN SOUL.
81. I FOLLOW MY HEART AND MY HEART LEADS THE WAY.
82. I AM TRUE TO MYSELF, AND OTHERS.
83. I BELIEVE BEFORE I RECEIVE.
84. I SEE THE FULFILLMENT OF MY MISSION.
85. I SEE MIRACLES IN MY LIFE.
86. THE WORDS THAT I SPEAK HAVE POWER.
87. I CREATE MY OWN EXPERIENCES.
88. I AM A CREATIVE CREATOR.
89. THIS TWIN SOUL LOVE IS TRUE.
90. AS I LOVE MYSELF UNCONDITIONALY I LOVE MY TWIN UNCONDITIONALY.
91. I CHOSE THIS JOURNEY AND HAVE THE POWER TO COMPLETE IT.
92. I AM RETURNING TO LOVE AND TAKING MY WINGS BACK.
93. I AM LOVED BY MY TWIN SOUL ALWAYS.
94. MY EYES WILL SEE WHAT MY HEART DESIRES.
95. I AM PEACEFUL.
96. EVERYTHING SERVES FOR MY HIGHEST GOOD.
97. I AM IN UNION.
98. I AM LOVED
99. I AM ENOUGH.
100. ALL IS WELL.

ENDING NOTE
(My wish for you dear reader)

My Dearest Reader and Beautiful Soul what is there to say in the end that I already haven't said; I love you and I am blessed with every soul who benefits from this book and comes just a bit more into unconditional love. I am blessed to know this twin soul love, and have this experience. I am blessed by the opportunity to share this experience with you. I am thankful for all of you who will be touched and come to an understanding of their own journey just a bit more through this book. For you who are on a journey with a soul mate I hope you recognize that embodying unconditional love will create beautiful evolved relationships in your life. These new reinvented relationships will be visible as we progress on our spiritual journeys.

I think we need these evolved relationships so we can nurture the hearts of our children in unconditional love, for the collective purpose of creating peace on this planet. Even if my sharing touches only one person, I feel like I have completed my mission. Thank you for taking this journey with me and for being brave to step up and follow your soul.

I will leave you now with the beautiful poem ' This is love' from one of my favourite poets, Rumi.

Love and light to you my beautiful soul

THIS IS LOVE

This is love: to fly toward a secret sky,
to cause a hundred veils to fall each moment.
First, to let go of life.
In the end, to take a step without feet;
to regard this world as invisible,
and to disregard what appears to be the self.

Heart, I said, what a gift it has been
to enter this circle of lovers,
to see beyond seeing itself,
to reach and feel within the breast.

GLOSSARY

ARCHETYPE- A recurring image or pattern of thinking which represents a typical human experience.

ASCENSION PROCESS- This is a process of alchemy, it is growing out of old systems of beliefs and moving your consciousness from a 'lower' reality of perceiving into the many possibilities and realities of existence. When we ascend, the perception and relationship with time and space changes. It means 'waking up' into your true self and remembering your divine origins.

AWAKENING- Means to awaken from the illusion of the false self into the limitless field of your true self.

BELIEF SYSTEM- Some beliefs in our lives are beneficial for our growth and well-being but most of our beliefs hinder and destroy our flow towards spiritual enlightenment. I call all of these sets of beliefs that have formed a fortress around your innocence 'self-belief systems'. Belief systems can be individual or collective.

CHAKRA- Chakras are energy wheels within our mortal bodies; you can imagine these wheels as swirling, and the faster they swirl the healthier our physical body. Mind, body and soul are intimately connected and if a disease manifests in the physical body chakras are usually on a slow spin or are blocked, as the life energy cannot go through and nourish the body and the organs.

COLLECTIVE UNCONSCIOUS- The deepest layer of the unconscious, which extends beyond the individual psyche.

CRYSTAL CHILD- They began to appear from the 1990s to 2010 and have a group consciousness tasked with revealing our inner power and bringing oneness on the planet. Their aura seems almost transparent, appearing as clear as crystal. They are clairvoyant and healing, very sensitive to the collective consciousness. They are empaths who avoid sharp sounds and dislike unnatural light, and they often speak about oneness and Divine love.

DIVINE LOVE- This is a state of awareness and consciousness where there is present unconditional love.

DUALITY- The quality or state of having or experiencing two states usually with the opposite meaning, for example, love/hate, light/dark, hot/cold, good/evil.

EGO MIND- The self-centred part of your conscious self that causes you to make choices based on how you are perceived by others or by your lower self that usually forms a layer or a shell to prevent you from connecting to your true self.

EMBODIED -To give a concrete form, express, personify.

EMPATH- Highly sensitive person who absorbs other peoples' emotions and/or physical symptoms. They have highly tuned senses.

FAMILY TEMPLATE- This is a pattern of behaviour or trauma that goes through your ancestors and family. This pattern then creates a template in the family line which can hinder your progress or make it difficult for you to move on in your life. This is called entanglement where your fate is linked with the unresolved difficult fate of someone else in your family system.

ILLUMINATION/HARMONIZING- It is a stage of internal harmony when physical reunion becomes possible depending on what both twins choose.

INCARNATED- (from the Latin 'incaro') – means 'in the flesh' or given a human form.

INITIATION OF SOUL- This is the 'spark' that lights the fire for the purpose of embarking on a spiritual quest. It is the touch of the mysterious, where you gain dominion over certain aspects of your lower nature and are called to 'step up 'and explore further into your own soul's journey.

INTUITIVE- Knowing things without having to reason them out.

INDIGO CHILD- These children being born since about 1970 are here on Earth to show humanity its true essence. Research of human auric fields showed that these children have a deep blue (indigo) aura. From an early age they are strong willed, very creative and always looking for ways to express their creative energy through poetry, writing, jewellery making and other artistic endeavours. They display 'old soul' characteristics even when young. Very intuitive and psychic, they are usually introverts who have a desire to help humanity in a major way. They bond easily with plants and animals. They don't accept rigid ritualistic rules and outdated concepts. They are somewhat like system busters where they change the status quo of things. They feel special from early childhood and know that they are on a 'mission'. They are here to break the old paradigm and open the way for the new.

HEART CHAKRA- The centre of unconditional love and compassion, the heart chakra is the centre of the human energy system.

KUNDALINI- This is a primal energy located at the base of the spine. It exists in everyone's body, usually in a dormant state and most people never know it is there and available for them. It is a vital force lying dormant until something triggers it to awaken, and this leads a person towards spiritual growth and eventually, enlightenment.

MERKABA- Mer-meaning Light, Ka-meaning Spirit, and Ba- meaning Body. Merkaba is a spirit body which transports spirit body from one dimension into another. It is a space/time dimension vehicle of ascension. Mer-ka-ba is situated around the human body like a sacred geometric web dormant and waiting to become activated.

OVER-SOUL- It is the concept that one universal spirit lives in all. Over-Soul is where all souls emanate from before embarking on this earthly journey. Over-soul is a spiritual unity of all souls and therefore transcends individual consciousness.

PINK BALLOON PHASE- This phase in the twin soul journey represents the time after the initial meeting of twins took place, up until the first separation in the physical. It is a phase of bliss between twins where within their souls, both twins see or get a glimpse into the beauty of real soul love.

PROJECTION- A process where an unconscious characteristic, a fault, or even a talent of one's own is seen as belonging to another person or object.

RADIANCE PHASE- This phase comes after the Surrender Phase when twins clearly see that this sacred love is not only about the two of them but is much more, it is about a mission. In this phase they start radiating their authenticity and doing their hearts' mission.

RAINBOW CHILD- These children are a third generation of special children embodied here on Earth to help humanity evolve. As the name implies their aura is a beautiful rainbow and they are very drawn to colour in all shapes and forms. They bring pure joy into their families, and are very conscious from an early age. They are psychic and natural born healers and creators, and are all about service and helping everybody around them. They are fearless and usually without karma. They have never been incarnated on Earth before and are here to finish what Indigos and Crystals have started. They are here to show us how to open our hearts fully and evolve to higher consciousness.

REPRESSED- Experiences that have been actively pushed out of the conscious mind into the unconscious .

SACRED RELATIONSHIPS- Relationships that we form with soul mates or twin souls from fifth dimensional awareness for the mutual highest possible evolution of souls. These relationships will be the norm of future relating between people and they are going to be karma free.

SHADOW- The unconscious part of the personality that contains characteristics which one cannot recognize as one's own.

SEPARATION PHASE- This is a phase in a twin soul journey where twin souls go their separate ways to learn, grow, and mature spiritually.

SEVEN CHAKRA SYSTEM- This is the template of seven bodily energy centres which are located inside the body from the base of the spine up to the crown.

SOUL FAMILY- The spiritual equivalent of your birth family here on earth. You share the same Over-soul with members of your soul family and their task is to help you with your soul purpose and accelerate your spiritual growth.

SOUL FREQUENCY- This is the exact frequency 'given' to a particular soul, in other words we could say that this is your soul name or soul signature.

SOURCE- This means God/ Goddess, Atman, Tao, Brahman, Divine, Universe, Higher power, Infinite intelligence.

SOUL MATE- Is a person with whom one has a feeling of deep natural affinity. Soul mates recognize each other for the purpose of fulfilling a certain task together in life.

SUBJECTIVE- Coming from the self.

SURRENDER PHASE- This is a phase in a twin soul journey where twin souls, after all the struggle, pain, and suffering, finally surrender this Union to the God/Goddess.

SYNCHRONICITY- The simultaneous occurrence of two meaningful but not causally connected events.

THIRD CHAKRA- The solar plexus is the seat of the soul and twin souls are joined at the soul. This is where the energy exchange between them takes place.

THE TWELVE CHAKRA SYSTEM- Brings forth the vision of our human connection to the entire Universe, these additional five chakras are outside the body, one below the root chakra and the surface of the earth, and the rest above the crown.

TWIN SOUL- Is when one soul is incarnated into two bodies for the purpose of experiencing life through two perspectives, the masculine and the feminine, in the same lifetime.

TWIN SOUL UNION- The Inner Marriage or Sacred Marriage is the union between the Masculine and the Feminine energies that are within us. It is the integration with the Christ self so that the twin soul union can happen in the physical.

UNCONSCIOUS- Parts of the mind and personality of which a person is unaware.

UNION- This means togetherness, or the non-separate state of two twin souls, the ultimate goal of a balanced and unconditional state of Divine love between the two. Unification of soul.

YING AND YANG- The two balances and opposite principles that operate in the universe.

3D- This is the three dimensional time and space perception where you can sequentially move your body in time and space. This is the material world in which we live. In this dimension energy is congested into a dense pool of matter. The perception in this dimension is confined to within our five senses which we have so that we can navigate through this dimension of reality. In this dimension humans suffer from the illusion of being separate from their Spirit and God/Goddess. This plane is a dimension of mind.

4D- The fourth dimension is the dimension of thought and time where we can time travel. Our mind can time travel here so that we can plan in life and make decisions. This dimension is also called the astral plane where we can research our soul journey and travel out of the body, aka astral travel. This is the dimension where magic, time travel, reincarnation, flying, enchantment and mind reading are all possible.

5D- The dimension of 'heaven' or light. Here in this dimension we base our decisions on love not fear, and we experience the oneness with our Father/Mother creator. You experience your life as a true miracle and see that your life is unfolding from your Spirit. You don't feel the walls of time/space limitation and you know that miracles are given to you freely. You feel your mission in contributing to humanity though your way of living and being, and you know that by remaining in love you can manifest miracles in your life and the lives of others.

ABOUT THE AUTHOR

Geraldina Lumezi is a spiritual teacher, counsellor, and life coach who holds diplomas in Hypnotherapy, PLT Therapy (past life regression), and Theta Therapy. She is a passionate advocate for the philosophy of the Twin Soul or Twin Flame connection, which is the old knowledge that at the dawn of time twin souls were one soul encompassing male and female energies in a single entity. Due to separation, twin souls experienced a split and thus are destined to search for each other through years and perhaps lifetimes until they finally come into union with each other.

As a spiritual teacher Geraldina feels that her life's purpose is bringing heart consciousness and help twin souls and soul mates to come into union and loving sacred relationships. Her own twin soul journey, which has endured for the past twenty three years, has enabled her to enhance her skills as an intuitive life coach and experienced twin soul spiritual counsellor for all who are on a quest for this union and who are in need of balance.

Geraldina is fascinated by the effects of altered states of human consciousness and her education in this field and past life regression work with clients has convinced her of the healing benefits exploration of the subconscious can have on human life and experience.
An therapist, author, poet and passionate reader, she is a lover of nature who enjoys music and embraces all of the myriad joys of life.

Contact author at: www.regresija-theta.com
                       www. twinsouleternallove.com

The path into unconditional love is born out of
More soul
More heart
More compassion
More peace

Made in the USA
Monee, IL
25 November 2019